# For Your Names' Sake

## A Father's Letter to His Children

By John D. Ramsey

John Ramsey is a husband of one, father of four, and jack of many trades. John currently works as a senior software engineer in the Kansas City area. He and his wife, Lisa, have been married since 1981. They live with their two younger children in a comfortable home on a quiet street in the little city of Raymore.

*For Your Names' Sake,*

*A Father's Letter to His Children*

Copyright © 2007 by John D. Ramsey, All rights reserved.
ISBN 978-0-6151-5651-4

Scripture designated NIV taken from the HOLY BIBLE, NEW INTERNATIONAL VERSION, Copyright © 1973, 1978, 1984 by International Bible Society. Used by permission of Zondervan Publishing House.

Scripture designated NASB taken from the NEW AMERICAN STANDARD BIBLE®, Copyright © 1960, 1962, 1963, 1968, 1971, 1972, 1973, 1975, 1977, 1995 by the Lockman Foundation. Used By Permission.

Scripture designated KJV taken from The Holy Bible, King James Version

# For Your Names' Sake,

## A Father's Letter to His Children

Chapter 1—The Glory of Man .................................................... 9

Chapter 2—The Fall of Man ..................................................... 17

Chapter 3—The Sacrifice of Christ ............................................ 51

Chapter 4—The Wrath of Man .................................................. 81

Chapter 5—The Resurrection ................................................. 105

Chapter 6—The Wrath of God ................................................ 125

Chapter 7—Today ................................................................ 137

# Dedication

*To Cara Michal:* You taught me joy. May you always be a little river of joy to people who know you, and may the Joy of the Lord flood your own soul as you grow in your knowledge of Him.

*To Daniel Shane:* You inspire me to be strong. You taught me to laugh at myself. In your dealings among men and women may you always remember that God is your only judge, and for all your life remember that God is gracious. May you always seek to please Him, and may his mercy and grace follow you all your days.

*To Claire Maddison:* You teach me boldness and perseverance. You are a bright and shining warrior. May you put on the full armor of God and stand firm in faith as you reflect to the world the light of God's truth.

*To Gabrielle Sophia:* You will always be my baby girl. You teach me gentleness. God in his great wisdom blessed this family with you long after we thought we were finished having children. May you always be a messenger of God's wisdom to everyone who knows you.

*To Lisa:* Thank you for 26 years of patience and love. Thank you for loving and nurturing our children. Thank you for always helping me. Thank you for encouraging this effort. Thank you for re-reading this text so many times as it matured. May God always bless you in our lives together and in the lives of our children.

## Repentance, Circa 1979

*On You, O Christ, the Cornerstone, I fall*
*To break my will; it is no longer mine.*
*I weary over living my design*
*And give to you a sacrifice, my all.*
*I listen for your gentle voice to call*
*Me to your humble service. Lord, incline*
*My heart to understand your every line*
*And precept. Then though I am very small*
*I may be used by you to do your will,*
*An honor not befitting any man*
*But still bestowed on those who dare to take*
*Your easy yoke and let your love instill*
*The burden and the strength to work your plan.*
*O Lord, see fit to use me for your sake.*

## CHAPTER 1—THE GLORY OF MAN

*"Pontiac!"*— Daniel age 3
*"Porsche..."*— Daniel age 10
*"Mirror, mirror, on the wall, who's the fairest of the **mall**?"*— Cara age 4

Dearest kids,

    We live in an amazing time. Yet we are rarely astonished. We witness modern miracles, but are mostly concerned with whether we can afford them, whether they are in stock, and whether to pay for overnight shipping. We experience daily what men in previous times could not even imagine, and we are not exhilarated. If we reflect, we might conjure some quiet amazement, some sentiment about how fortunate we are or about how different our lives are from men and women in history. So that is where I'll begin: with a reflection on how utterly amazing our lives are. Try not to yawn; it gets better.

    As I begin writing this book, I am also working a contract in downtown Minneapolis. I will not be on that contract for much longer so I will try to write fast. Anyway, my day begins sometime before 6:00 AM when the alarm clock goes off and I turn on lights and bathe in hot running water. Once dressed, I put on my glasses and insert my hearing aid. Your mother grinds coffee beans imported from Peru or Tanzania (whichever is available). She always makes my coffee and packs my lunch. Some mornings she even fixes me breakfast. I walk out the door carrying my thermal mug, my lunch bag, and my *Wall Street Journal*.

# Chapter 1

I drive about two thirds of the distance to Minneapolis, park at Fort Snelling, and board the LRT, or *Light Rail Transit*. Along the way to the fort, I sometimes wonder about the technology that makes this all possible. I know a little about cars and engines. I have done minor repairs, but mostly I take for granted that the Explorer will start. I expect that it will transport me in relative safety to my destination regardless of snow or ice during Minnesota winters. Driving the Explorer would be unpleasant or impossible without the streets and roads built and maintained by the city, county, and state departments of transportation. I traverse several bridges; the most amazing on my route is over the Minnesota River. Its arches support 4 lanes of traffic and a bicycle trail (who would have the nerve to bicycle across that bridge?). The river basin and wildlife area are 60 to 80 feet below, and the bridge itself appears to stretch across the valley for nearly a mile.

I wonder sometimes what Pharaoh would have thought about my Ford Explorer. Would he trade me for a horse and a golden chariot? (Answer: Yes, until he saw a Lexus). What would Caesar have thought about Minnesota highways and bridges? Surely Roman road builders are no match for MN/DOT's civil engineers. What would either Pharaoh or Caesar think about the aircraft I watch taking off and landing at MSP? What would they think about the Twin Cities' skylines visible to the northwest and northeast as I cross the bridge?

Before I board the LRT, I buy a ticket at a vending machine using my American Express card. I do not always think about how far my credit information must travel and how quickly it must return for the ticket machine to approve the purchase and print my ticket and receipt. Sometimes I do think about the impact of technology because I am a geek. However, in everyday life it is commonplace, even mundane. Technology does not astonish me. I just hope my card is authorized and my ticket is printed before the train leaves the station. I always keep dollar coins in my pocket just in case the transaction processing fails.

While zipping past the cars on Hiawatha, I can use my phone to send text messages, send or receive email, view news highlights on msnbc.com, or to play Jawbreaker or Solitaire. I can even use my phone to play music like Bob Dylan, James Taylor, and Pink Floyd. My phone understands my

## The Glory of Man

handwriting. It has a built-in camera with video. I also have seven translations of the Bible on my phone, although I only use three or four.

With my Pocket PC phone from Sprint, I can talk to any of you for an unlimited time for no additional cost regardless of how far away you might be. I can do all this while riding the LRT to Government Plaza where the doors open automatically and the passengers spill onto the platform and dissipate into the towers and skyways of Minneapolis.

After exiting the train, I enter the skyway, walk a few blocks, and board an elevator that deposits me a few steps from my desk. If all goes well I might even be the first one there and enjoy a few moments of solitude before the stress of the day begins.

I wonder sometimes whether we really understand how amazing our modern culture and society really is. The ancient civilizations around the Mediterranean Sea learned to build ships and transport people and cargo throughout the region. If they traded with the Far East, however, they used overland routes. What do you think; would FedEx humiliate them?

Sometimes while waiting at Fort Snelling for the train I can hear the turboprops of the Air Guard taking off and landing in the fog. For centuries, men have navigated by the sun and the stars. What would the ancients think about GPS? How would we describe to them a manmade constellation? I keep trying to figure out why I *need* to have a GPS device. I like technology. I am a geek.

We are technology savvy people. When we compare ourselves to our ancestors, we handicap history; we give it an advantage. The ancients are amazing not because of what they accomplished but because they accomplished it without modern tools and technology; good for them. Modern man is even more amazing because of the tools and technologies he has assembled and organized. Modern man accomplishes a greater volume of work in a shorter period. We have made a science of just about everything, and everything moves faster than ever before.

Modern man has amassed more wealth than was ever imagined by Nebuchadnezzar. Moreover, it is not the property of kings. It belongs to free men everywhere. Economists tell us that wealth potential is limitless with free markets in free and secure societies. Men do not become rich at others' expense, because one man's wealth generates wealth for others, too. The

# Chapter 1

economic cycle lifts many more out of poverty. So three cheers for modern man and for everything we have accomplished. Congratulations for all we know, and for all we can claim as our own.

The Hubble Space Telescope has peered further into the night than Galileo ever dreamed. As a child, I watched television as men walked on the moon. Space Shuttles have flown into space on and off for decades. A few years ago, SpaceShipOne flew to space and back twice within a week powered by $NO_2$ and rubber cement. Nitrous oxide and rubber cement do not sound very high tech to us. Coffee bars use $NO_2$ to charge the whipped cream dispensers. Rubber cement is fast-drying glue that once upon a time was used to composite elements of page layouts. It holds things temporarily and cleans up quickly when dry. These mundane compounds together propelled a rocket plane to space. They indicate how commonplace space travel will become in the not-too-distant future. That, in fact, was the point of SpaceShipOne: to show that space travel may be more accessible than NASA has allowed it to become.

We have radios, and televisions, DVDs, TiVo, iPods and MP3 players, mobile phones, and laser pointers (how cool are laser pointers?). We have Internet, high-speed Internet, wireless Internet, high-speed wireless Internet: all realized within the last few decades. We have Internet on mobile phones. We have Google! We have Google on our phones (text message your questions to 46645 and Google will text message you back with an answer)!

People are glorious beings. Our creations reflect our glory: our achievements, technologies, and art declare how amazing we truly are. We are unparalleled among all other creatures on the Earth past and present. We have eclipsed even the imaginations of the ancients.

We have taken all the knowledge of the ages and we have capitalized it. We have made it accessible, affordable, convenient, and marketable. We have made it common. We can listen to Bob Dylan playing from devices in our pockets while riding a train past Dinky Town. Dylan knew that times were *changin'*; did he imagine that the world would become what it is today?

The achievements of the ancients pale in comparison to our own. What have they accomplished that modern man has not bettered? They remind us of *Ozymandius*, the sonnet by Percy Bysshe Shelley.

# The Glory of Man

> I met a traveler from an antique land
> Who said:—Two vast and trunkless legs of stone
> Stand in the desert. Near them on the sand,
> Half sunk, a shatter'd visage lies, whose frown
> And wrinkled lip and sneer of cold command
> Tell that its sculptor well those passions read
> Which yet survive, stamp'd on these lifeless things
> The hand that mock'd them and the heart that fed.
> And on the pedestal these words appear:
> "My name is Ozymandius, king of kings:
> Look on my works, ye mighty, and despair!"
> Nothing beside remains: round the decay
> Of that colossal wreck, boundless and bare,
> The lone and level sands stretch far away.[i]

Perhaps we are rightfully smug amidst all the glories of modern man. Perhaps more than any other age, we know the transience of our own creation. We should follow Shelley's advice and look upon our own works and despair. We despair not because Ozymandius' works are greater, but because we know how temporal our glory really is. The more we create, the more evident is the accelerated obsolescence of our own creation. Surely iPods and Blackberries and even Pocket PCs with phones will be bested by something else, and sooner than we think.

The fleets of all the airlines are now obsolesced by the mere promise of the Boeing 787 and 777. The original Airbus A350 design was kaput before it was prototyped. We modern men have the ultimate luxury of viewing yesterday's miracles with either contempt or nostalgia. We no sooner acquire something new before we covet something newer. Our economy depends on the never-ending cycle of obsolescence and upgrade. We are undaunted by change because we have learned that change is opportunity. Someday we will trade in our gas guzzling Explorer for some super-efficient hybrid. The automobile manufacturers will adapt by building more sophisticated power systems. The oil companies will adapt by developing alternative fuels. The consumer will continue to buy whatever pleases him.

Look around you; we are a paper plate culture. We use and discard without thinking. We seldom master a technology; rather the pursuit of change masters us. What we have lost in this cyclone of discard-and-upgrade is any sense of permanence. No wonder our *amazing* technologies leave us yawning. They are exhausting.

Our greatest achievements eventually become commodity products, and commodities are boring. In Pixar's *The Incredibles*[ii], Syndrome, the arch villain is not a *super*. Rather he is a weapons engineer turned ugly. He sets out to destroy all the superheroes. Lacking any superpowers of his own, he creates machines to simulate super-human strength. Syndrome eventually plans to sell his technology so that everyone can be super. He observes with vitriol, "When everyone is super, then no one will be." Such is the course of our best creations. On their way to obsolescence, they become commodity products. They become accessible, commonplace, and consequently they are no longer amazing.

Technology is not the only dimension of modern life that lacks permanence. Our heroes and leaders have also become disposable. Robert Frost (1874-1963) noticed this cultural phenomenon when he wrote his poem *Provide, Provide*:

> The picture pride of Hollywood
> Too many fall from great to good
> For you to doubt the likelihood.[iii]

Frost's smug irony deflates our egos as he puts smiles on our faces.

General Douglas MacArthur famous for his victorious campaign against Japan in WWII and his contributions to the successful re-engineering of Japanese society is often remembered for his speech before Congress where he said, "Old soldiers never die; they just fade away." Nevertheless, in our super-disposable society, disgrace and scandal frequently replace graceful exits such as MacArthur's.

Ronald Reagan may be the last US president remembered as a great man. With the current speed of information, no man's character and reputation can withstand the immediate and comprehensive scrutiny of modern newsgathering and distribution. Today's greatest men await their own public disgrace brought about by the disclosure that they are fallible.

Obsolescence is an unpleasant fact. We fight to remain relevant, but we lose our edge. We hope to become wiser as our wits become dimmer, but with

## The Glory of Man

the pace of changing culture, our wisdom soon lacks the perspective to provide value. Bruce Springsteen laments in an *old* song:

>Glory days, well; they'll pass you by,
>
>Glory days, in the wink of a young girl's eye,
>
>Glory days, glory days.[iv]

Our creations are temporary, and we are temporary. Our great inventions end up in landfills or recycling bins. Our elderly end up in nursing facilities. The wise old men who in past centuries would have sat at the city gates, now sit in sterile plastic lounges watching daytime TV. What reasonable hope do we have to avoid a fate of irrelevance? "Too many fall from great to good, for you to doubt the likelihood."

Although computers are the new thing, I have no expectation that my knowledge of computers will retain value in my old age. I no longer program the way I did even a couple years ago. In fact, the systems that are a few years old are called *legacy* systems. They no longer correspond well with the business enterprise processes and will constantly need updating until they can be replaced.

Near the end of 1999 as businesses were wrapping up their Y2K initiatives, I saw a middle-aged man in business attire standing on the street corner holding a sign that read, "Will program COBOL Y2K for food." This was morbidly funny because in 1999, unemployment was still high and too many people were on the streets holding signs declaring, "Will do any work for food."

COBOL was once a common business programming language. It has largely been supplanted by Java and .NET programming languages. By the end of 1999, the last major revisions to old COBOL systems were being finished and COBOL programming skills were becoming more difficult to market. While the job seeker's methodology was intent upon eliciting smiles, it nonetheless demonstrated that possessing only unneeded skills makes a man as vulnerable as having no skills.

What becomes of us when our talents are no longer valuable? What has become of all the telephone operators, railroad brakeman, the typesetters and lithographers, and the COBOL programmers? Where are they now? James, the brother of Jesus, tells us, "For the sun rises with a scorching wind and withers the grass; and its flower falls off and the beauty of its appearance is

# Chapter 1

destroyed; so too the rich man in the midst of his pursuits will fade away."[1] James' words are ever true today.

What if our most glorious accomplishments, while memorable, turn tragic? In the early 20th Century, few men were as inspired or as inspiring as T. E. Lawrence, aka *Lawrence of Arabia*. Lawrence was instrumental in helping the British Army defeat the Turks. Under British and French administration, Arab nations eventually became self-governing. While Lawrence's exploits changed the world, they brought with them unintended consequences. Without the secular (and absolute) rule of the Ottoman Empire, the Middle East is now disintegrating into a maelstrom of religious fascism.

Israel, which emerged from British oversight as a shining example of freedom and justice, is now hated by its neighbors and by most of the governments of the world. Nearly 100 years later, Lawrence's accomplishments are difficult for peace-loving men to celebrate. It is doubtful that T. E. Lawrence as a Lieutenant in the British Army understood what he was unleashing upon the world. Whatever he accomplished, the subsequent history of bloodshed has tarnished his memory.

Perhaps I am too hard on Lawrence. Perhaps the British should have allowed Arab independence sooner rather than later. Perhaps exploitation and interference sowed the seeds of corruption. Nevertheless, Lawrence of Arabia demonstrates that man cannot always control what he creates. Nor can he control his own fate: Thomas Edward Lawrence, military genius and political idealist, died from a motorcycle accident in 1935 and is buried in Dorset, England.

Nothing that we are, nothing we do, and nothing we create survives the passage of time. Yes, we are glorious creatures; our creations and our conquests reflect our glory, *and* they reflect our frailty and impermanence. Our toys, tools, and trinkets obsolesce or break. Our victories turn into defeat. We die, and we can control none of it.

What is wrong with mankind?

---

[1] James 1:11 (NASB)

# CHAPTER 2—THE FALL OF MAN

*"What's wrong with Smurfs?"*— Daniel age 4
*"When I'm five, I'm going to be a teenager."*— Cara age 4
*"I just blessed myself three times . . .*
*. . . and now my hands are sticky."* — Gabby age 4

We really do not need Shelley, or Frost, or even Springsteen to make the point for our transience and obsolescence. We do not need to reflect on our computers, our mobile phones, or even yesterday's *Wall Street Journal* to understand it. Nor is it a strictly modern phenomenon although modern culture accelerates the process. King Solomon, a long time ago, dedicated the whole book of Ecclesiastes to the topic. He said,

> "Meaningless! Meaningless!"
> Says the Teacher.
> "Utterly meaningless!
> Everything is meaningless."[2]

Solomon's thesis is a little alarming; especially if you thought that the Bible was a motivational book. Solomon declares out loud what we all know in our hearts. Death robs life of its meaning. As Solomon examined man's glory, he finds purpose in one thing:

> Remember him—before the silver cord is severed,
> Or the golden bowl is broken,

---

[2] Ecclesiastes 1:2 (NIV)

# Chapter 2

> Before the pitcher is shattered at the spring,
> Or the wheel is broken at the well,
> and the dust returns to the
> Ground it came from,
> And the spirit returns to God who gave it.
> "Meaningless! Meaningless!" Says the Teacher.
> "Everything is meaningless!"
> . . . Of making books there will be no end,
> And much study wearies the body.
> Now all has been heard;
> **Here is the conclusion of the matter:**
> **Fear God and keep his commandments,**
> **For this is the whole duty of man.**
> **For God will bring every deed into judgment,**
> **Including every hidden thing,**
> **Whether it is good or evil.**[3]

What does Solomon mean, "Before the silver cord is severed, the golden bowl is broken, the pitcher is shattered at the spring, or the wheel is broken at the well?" What are those word pictures supposed to mean? Some people think these objects have special symbolic significance: silver cord, golden bowl, pitcher, and wheel at the well. Perhaps Solomon somehow understood them as euphemisms of our lives and deaths. Reading them again, I think they are our creations, our trophies, our art, our tools, our machines. They fail, disappoint, obsolesce, and break. Our bodies return to dust and our spirits return to God. Before that happens, Solomon tells us to do something: fear and obey God.

The nature of man is complex. We are amazing, gifted, talented, intelligent, creative, but we are also broken and decaying. Our glory contrasts with our frailty. When an artist captures the essence of both our glory and our frailty, we call it Shakespearian.

Robert Frost's poem titled *Out, Out* begins, "The buzz-saw snarled and rattled in the yard . . ." Frost captures an ominous tone in the first line. The story will not work out well; we can tell immediately. Within the narrative,

---
[3] Ecclesiastes 12:6-8, 12-14 (NIV)

# The Fall of Man

the imperfection of man's creation and the frailty of a boy's life collide in tragedy (almost Shakespearian). The poem ends:

> They listened at his heart.
> Little-less-nothing! and that ended it.
> No more to build on there. And they, since they
> Were not the one dead, turned to their affairs.[v]

Frost's title, *Out, Out*, is an allusion to Shakespeare's *Macbeth*.

> Out, out, brief candle!
> Life's but a walking shadow, a poor player
> that struts and frets his hour upon the stage
> and then is heard no more.
> It is a tale told by an idiot,
> full of sound and fury,
> signifying nothing.[vi]

Perhaps this line is a bit of self-deprecating humor from Shakespeare; nonetheless, Macbeth did not live happily ever after. After Macbeth achieves success through treachery, fear and guilt drive him insane. He ends up paying for his crimes with his head. Our own stories are not so different. Often our own bad decisions bring to us our greatest hardships.

Regardless, modern man is most glorious. He can treat and cure diseases with medical treatments and devices he has invented, but he can also kill with the powerful weapons he designs. Both reveal man's glorious creativity. Yes, even our weapons are glorious. We can take into the palm of our hand the power of an ancient army. We can wield this power for sport and recreation, for self-defense, for destruction, and even for self-destruction. Our nation has weapons amazing for both their power and precision. Our military is unparalleled. We can deliver *shock and awe* at anytime in any place.

GPS might help an aircraft land safely in the fog, thereby protecting the passengers on board, or it might guide a missile to its target. Perhaps the missile kills hoards of evil men intent on harming others. Perhaps it is good we have smart bombs and missiles, but the reasons we need them is evidence enough that man is broken. With the glory of our technology, we can wage war half a world away. Man can make glorious war, but he cannot maintain simple peace.

# Chapter 2

The death of man is certain. Everyone cured from cancer will die of something. Non-smokers do not have a lower mortality rate than smokers. Both have mortality rates of roughly 100%.

We have the most incredible capability with modern medicine (although we cannot always afford it). We can defibrillate, intubate, and resuscitate to save a life. Do we really save life? Our most noble efforts can prolong life, but they do not prevent death. We claim that medical science saves lives, but truthfully, the best it can accomplish is to heal present diseases, repair certain injuries, and postpone death. In some sad cases, medicine can only prolong the process of dying. Medical science may be noble, but the sadness of watching a loved one die slowly demonstrates medicine's futility. Given enough time, we will all die, and in time, everything will be forgotten. Everything we know will be surpassed. Everything we build will be destroyed,

What do we call surviving examples of ancient architecture? We call them *ruins*. The people who built the ruins were skilled artisans of their day. Maybe they were famous. Today they are mostly anonymous, forgotten, and they are entirely dead. Every man can look forward to this. "Look on my works, ye mighty, and despair!" Ozymandius proclaims, but his works are now rubble. We need not fear Ozymandius, but we, too, will join him in death as our mighty works crumble. This gives us more reason to despair; we fear our own demise.

So we live and we die, but eventual death is not our only sadness. During our short lives, we also have troubles and fears. We seek peace and safety, but we have neither. We move to the countryside to avoid the violence of the city, but we travel highways on which we all assume responsibility for our safety and the safety of others. Each day we pass memorials to those killed in automobile accidents: accidents wherein man or machine failed in its responsibility to protect life.

Children are not safe, though we advocate child safety. Some children are not safe in the city, some are not safe at school, some are not safe with friends, some are not safe with relatives, some are not safe at church, and some are not even safe at home. We seek peace and safety, but can we find it?

When Daniel was two-years old, we let him play outside in the back yard while the windows of the house were open. In time, we heard him yelling frantically and went out to find that he had hung himself on the ornamental

# The Fall of Man

detail on the top of the gate. Failing to open the gate, he had decided to climb over. The gate designed to protect him could have destroyed him.

I have quizzed you kids asking, "Where is the safest place to be during a California earthquake?" You know the answer, it's *Kansas*, but Kansas has tornados, lightening, and stifling heat. There comes a place where no amount of insulation will protect us. We seek peace and safety, but it is an illusion. There may be degrees of conflict and danger, but there is no such thing as peace and safety.

Our hearts desire justice (a prerequisite for peace), nevertheless, some evil men go unpunished while others are punished for non-existent crimes or for crimes committed by others. With man's best efforts for justice, injustice abounds. The United States executes justice as a process. Even when the process works according to design, injustice persists. We hold on to the process because without it, injustice would consume us all.

Why is man such an amazing creature? Why is man such a broken creature? The book of Genesis answers these questions.

> Then God said, "Let us make man in our image, in our likeness, and let them rule over the fish of the sea and the birds of the air, over the livestock, over all the earth, and over all the creatures that move along the ground."
> So God created man in his own image.[4]

We are amazing creatures, and consequently we are amazing creators because the Creator made us in his image. He intended us to be amazing. This all overwhelmed David. He asked God,

> What is man that you are mindful of him,
> the son of man that you care for him?
> You made him a little lower than the heavenly beings
> and crowned him with glory and honor.
> You made him ruler over the works of your hands;
> you put everything under his feet:[5]

Although this prophecy will ultimately be fulfilled in Jesus Christ (according to Hebrews 2), this position of honor is also where God put Adam and Eve in the beginning. God blessed them and said to them, "Be fruitful and increase

---

[4] Genesis 1:26-27 (NIV)
[5] Psalm 8:4-6 (NIV)

in number; fill the earth and subdue it. Rule over the fish of the sea and the birds of the air and over every living creature that moves on the ground."[6]

The creation of man was intimate and personal. In the creation, God spoke things into existence:

Let there be light . . . Let there be an expanse between the waters . . . Let dry land appear . . . Let the land produce vegetation . . . Let there be lights in the expanse of the sky . . . Let the waters teem with living creatures . . . Let the land produce living creatures . . . Let us make man in our image. (NIV)

Creation comes by the word of his mouth until he says, "Let us make man in our image." At this point, the method of creation takes a more personal direction. Moses explains, "The LORD God formed the man from the dust of the ground and breathed into his nostrils the breath of life, and the man became a living being."[7]

All creation was designed and effected by God, but God specially, personally, and physically formed the first man from the dust of the ground. Creation of man was up close and personal! God sculpted man in clay after his own likeness. God then breathed into man's nostrils the breath of life. If you symbolize this, generalize this, spiritualize this, or by any other means diminish this, you miss an important point. When Adam first opened his eyes, he looked upon the face of his Creator. A Creator that appeared immediately familiar to Adam; having the same hands, feet, eyes, mouth, and lips as Adam had. Adam was made in the image of the Creator. All the other animals were interesting and diverse, but Adam was made in the perfect likeness of his Creator.

God made Adam in his image; however, Adam was not a god nor was he an extension or duplication of God. He was in every way accountable to God just as we also are. While Adam saw his Creator in physical form, God is not a physical being. He is spirit. God revealed himself to Adam in the physical realm, and the stature of a man still in some way reflects the nature of his Creator. In the Old Testament God appears in nature as a cloud, a pillar of fire, a burning bush, and as a man. God never appears as a species of animal, nor does he ever appear as a woman.

---

[6] Genesis 1:28 (NIV)
[7] Genesis 2:7 (NIV)

# The Fall of Man

Created in the image of his Creator, Adam was unique. This was not some detached, impersonal, or eventual creation. As this happened, the Creator was down in the dust forming the man in his own image and breathing into his nostrils the breath of life. God accomplished on the sixth day what no human artist can. As the Creator breathed, his sculpture transformed into living flesh, as the Creator breathed, the man's lungs inflated, his heart began beating, his eyes opened, his muscles flexed, and he became alive.

To understand how the creation was accomplished it helps to understand that God describes himself in three persons: the Father, Son, and Holy Spirit. God, the Father, resides on his throne in heaven and demonstrates the will of God and the omniscience (all-knowingness) of the Godhead. The Holy Spirit is everywhere throughout all creation (heaven and earth) and demonstrates the omnipresence and the power of the Godhead. The Son is the Creator God, and is the person of the Godhead who interacts with his creation. At various times, men have seen the Son in physical form. In the Garden of Eden, Adam and Eve did not walk with an ethereal presence, or cosmic fog. They walked with a person who looked like them, walked like them, and talked like them.

In Creation, all members of the Godhead are active. The Father willed it, the Spirit empowered it, and the Son performed it. The Son, who in the New Testament, became the man, Jesus Christ; in the Old Testament, reveals himself in many different places. There are several occurrences of the phrase, "the LORD appeared to . . ." These appearances were not mystical auras of Hollywood smoke and lights, but the human-like figure of the Son of God. In fact, it is misleading to say that the Son of God appears to be human-like when the reflexive is truer. Man is God-like. We are quickened sculptures of clay in the physical likeness that he chose as the representation of his nature. He is the original and eternal Creator God; we are human reflections of the original. John writes,

> In the beginning was the Word, and the Word was with God, and
> the Word was God. He was with God in the beginning. Through
> him all things were made; without him nothing was made that has
> been made. In him was life, and that life was the light of men.

## Chapter 2

The Word became flesh and made his dwelling among us. We have seen his glory, the glory of the One and Only, who came from the Father, full of grace and truth.

No one has ever seen God, but God the One and Only, who is at the Father's side, has made him known.[8]

The Son of God, the Word, is the Creator God; he is also Jesus, the Christ. No one has ever seen God the Father, but God the Son, Jesus Christ, has appeared to men and made the Father known. When people in the Old Testament including Adam and Eve interacted with God, they interacted with God, the Son. Hebrews, too, is emphatic about the Son's participation in Creation, ". . . in these last days [God] has spoken to us by his Son, whom he has appointed heir of all things, and through whom he made the universe."[9] When you stare at the expanse of the sky on a starry night, the Son of God created it. When you watch the ocean waves, or stand in front of a mountain, the Son of God designed it. When you look at the structure of life and living things, the Son of God fashioned it. When man took his first breath, the Son of God imparted it.

In the Old Testament the most revered name of God was simply, "I AM." This is the first and most important thing man must know about God: that he is! When God called Moses to deliver Israel, Moses saw several obstacles in the process. One of the obstacles was the name of God. Moses imagined that when he told the people of Israel that the God of their ancestors had sent him, they would ask, "Oh, yeah? What is his name?" God replied,

"I AM THAT I AM: and he said, Thus shalt thou say unto the children of Israel, 'I AM hath sent me unto you.'"

And God said moreover unto Moses, "Thus shalt thou say unto the children of Israel, 'the LORD God of your fathers, the God of Abraham, the God of Isaac, and the God of Jacob, hath sent me unto you: this is my name for ever, and this is my memorial unto all generations.'"[10]

In the Old Testament when the word *LORD* appears with small caps it means "I AM." In other words, God told Moses to tell the Israelites, "The I AM God of your fathers . . . has sent me to you."

---

[8] John 1:1-4, 14, 18 (NIV)
[9] Hebrews 1:2 (NIV)
[10] Exodus 3:14-15 (KJV)

## The Fall of Man

Jesus, rebuking the Jews, told them, "Your father Abraham rejoiced at the thought of seeing my day; he saw it and was glad."

The Jews answered, "You are not yet fifty years old, and you have seen Abraham!" Jesus then responded with something that had to be either blasphemy or true. He left no room for interpretation, equivocation, or alternative explanation. He said, "I tell you the truth, before Abraham was born, I AM!"[11] This declaration reverberated in the Jews' memory all the way back to the revelation of God's name to Moses. They picked up stones to kill Jesus, but he slipped away. They understood him as clearly as he intended them to understand: He was the Creator God, the God of Abraham, Isaac, and Jacob. He was the God that led them out of Egypt: the very God they claimed to worship in the Temple. Here Jesus was, standing in front of devoutly religious men, claiming for himself the most sacred name of God.

It is one thing to make bold claims, it is quite another to back it up with action. When an athlete is full of bravado, someone might tell him to "put up or shut up." God knew that Jesus' claim needed authentication. John continues the narration in chapter 9, Jesus leaves the Temple grounds, and

> ... As he went along, he saw a man blind from birth. His disciples asked him, "Rabbi, who sinned, this man or his parents that he was born blind?"
>
> "Neither this man nor his parents sinned," said Jesus, "but this happened so that the work of God might be displayed in his life. As long as it is day, we must do the work of him who sent me. Night is coming, when no one can work; while I am in the world, I am the light of the world."
>
> Having said this, he spit on the ground, made some mud with the saliva, and put it on the man's eyes. "Go," he told him, "wash in the Pool of Siloam" (this means Sent). So the man went and washed, and came home seeing.[12]

This is an amazing account, but we can miss the full drama because it is understated. An imposed chapter break between John 8 and 9 discourages connection, too. What Jesus did was this: In front of the very religious Jews,

---

[11] John 8:56-58 (NIV)
[12] John 9:1-6 (NIV)

he claimed to be *the* Creator God, the "I AM," whom they worshipped. In front of his disciples, he proved it.

This authenticating miracle needed to be one that only God could accomplish. Jesus healed other blind men, which indicated that he was the Messiah. The Jews were anticipating the coming of Messiah as a king, but they did not necessarily anticipate that he would be divine. Here Jesus proved that he was Messiah and God.

When we read John 9 this is what we are supposed to understand: Jesus took the dust of the ground and created new eyes for a man who had been born blind. After claiming to be Creator God, he demonstrated that he was Creator God. Jesus took the substance of earth and transformed it into living human tissue, a new creation so to speak, a creation that was no longer blind.

Jesus said that the man's blindness happened ". . . so that the work of God might be displayed in his life." What is the work of God? *Jesus' compassion for a man born blind demonstrates God's work of **creation**, his work of **redemption**, and his work of **reconciliation**.*

The healing created quite a kerfuffle with the Jews, and they threw the healed man out of the temple synagogue. Jesus heard this and went to find the man ". . . and when he found him, he said, 'Do you believe in the Son of Man?'"

"Who is he, sir? The man asked. "Tell me so that I may believe in him."

Jesus said, "You have now seen him; in fact, he is the one speaking with you."

The man said, "Lord, I believe," and he worshipped him.[13]

The man born blind and given sight by Jesus now sees his Creator in much the same manner that the first man did, and seeing him, he worships him. Jesus claimed to be Creator God, and then demonstrated that he was indeed the Creator God. After restoring sight for the man, Jesus then reveals himself, and the man responds in faith worshiping his Creator, his Healer, and his Redeemer. Jesus receives worship from the man: worship that was rightfully his because he is God. While the blind man could now see both physical and spiritual realms, the Jews who had no problems with their eyes, were blinded in their hearts.

---

[13] John 9:36-38 (NIV)

# The Fall of Man

The Jews of Jesus' time are not the only ones who are blinded to Jesus' identity. Christians, too, sometimes do not understand that the Son of God is also the Creator God. Claire's teacher asked in Sunday school, "Who created everything on the earth?" Claire answered with the faith of a child, "Jesus."

The teacher responded, "Well, not exactly. It was God." Nevertheless, Scripture is clear. The Son of God was physically active in Creation. Christians who believe that the universe and life evolved and that God was distant and detached disparage their Creator and their Savior.

I have always loved William Blake's poem, The Lamb, because it unapologetically explains in a child's voice and with a child's faith that the Creator God became the incarnate God-Man, the Lamb of God.

> Little Lamb, who made thee?
> Doest thou know who made thee?
> Gave thee life and bid thee feed.
> By the stream and o'er the mead;
> Gave thee clothing of delight,
> Softest clothing woolly bright;
> Gave thee such a tender voice.
> Making all the vales rejoice:
> Little Lamb who made thee?
> Doest thou know who made thee?
> Little Lamb I'll tell thee,
> Little Lamb I'll tell thee;
> He is called by thy name,
> For he calls himself a Lamb:
> He is meek and he is mild,
> He became a little child
> I a child and thou a lamb,
> We are called by His name,
> Little Lamb God bless thee,
> Little Lamb God bless thee.[vii]

The Son of God was personally involved in Creation. John says, "Through him all things were made; without him nothing was made that has been made."[14] Hebrews says, ". . . in these last days he [God] has spoken to us

---

[14] John 1:3 (NIV)

through his Son, whom he appointed heir of all things, and through whom he made the universe."[15] The Son of God, the Word, Jesus Christ was specifically, personally, and physically involved with the creation of man. The Creator made man as his image or reflection, and the Creator breathed into man the breath of life. The Father and the Holy Spirit are both involved in Creation and Redemption. Nevertheless, the Son of God is principally active in Creation and Redemption. The Son physically interacts with and intercedes for his Creation. It is important to understand that the Son of God is our Creator before we examine his role as our Redeemer.

We miss this truth sometimes (this is an understatement). Perhaps we imagine a distant and distracted deity. Perhaps we would prefer a God who was not so intimately aware of us, but he is aware. He formed the first man in clay and then instilled in him the breath of God. He is equally aware of each of us. David proclaimed,

> Where can I go from your Spirit?
> Or where can I flee from Your presence?
> If I ascend to heaven, You are there;
> If I make my bed in Sheol, behold, You are there.
> If I take the wings of dawn,
> If I dwell in the remotest part of the sea,
> Even there Your hand will lead me,
> And your right hand will lay hold of me.[16]

God, who created man in an intimate and personal manner, remains fully aware and involved with his creation. Hebrews says, "Nothing in all creation is hidden from God's sight. Everything is uncovered and laid bare before the eyes of him to whom we must give account."[17] God is not disinterested in man. He is intimately involved in the affairs of every man.

One night, as this book was in edit, Daniel called from two states away. He was sick and miserable and did not quite know what to do. Living on his own he had not acquired all the medical necessities that he might otherwise have had living with Mom and Dad. Realizing that he did not have the over-the-counter remedies that he needed Lisa began calling pharmacies near Daniel's house. She finally found one that was open and that would still

---

[15] Hebrews 1:2 (NIV)
[16] Psalm 139:7-10 (NASB)
[17] Hebrews 4:13(NIV)

# The Fall of Man

deliver that evening. Although 500 miles separated her from her child, nothing would stop her from getting him the care he needed. Nevertheless, God is much more interested in those who call him Father! Through his awesome power, he made us, and by his word, he sustains us. We are wonderfully made and especially loved.

Because the Creator formed man in the image of God, man is also capable of amazing things. We should not discount or dismiss man's glory and stature in creation. We are amazing. Our creations reflect our glory just as we, as his creations, reflect God's glory. We have our technology and our art as examples of our creativity. I have encouraged you children to learn technology. I have predicted that in future job markets there will be artists and geeks, and the artists will be geeks. Technology fully saturates most professional endeavors from business to manufacturing to medicine. Even our art depends upon modern technology.

Sometimes we take the opportunity to reflect on artwork created by primitive mediums such as brush on canvas. Sometimes we take the time to go to a gallery just to feel connected to something non-digital or *real* again. We might be disappointed to learn that modern painting, even abstract works, can be composed as electronic images before being committed to canvas. I once spoke with an artist during a studio open house. She had several collages of photocopied, black and white photographs. The arrangement of shapes juxtaposed manmade elements and natural organic elements evoking a spatial balance.

On the surface, they might have appeared to be the work of a 4-year-old child who had been left alone with scissors and glue. Nevertheless, the photocopies were not finished pieces. They were inspirations for boldly colored acrylic abstracts. The finished work would not reveal the technology behind the process, but technology played an essential role.

Few artists are truly purists in their chosen medium. They are like the rest of us; they understand the benefits of technology. Technology puts us at the pinnacle of our ability to create. We can expedite design, logistics, and manufacturing all by means of our technology. What we create today to increase productivity threatens to marginalize us tomorrow. With technology, the merely capable can compete with the truly gifted, and both will have a very short season under the sun before a better tool or someone more proficient supersedes them. As technology triumphs, the individual becomes less relevant. His own inventions displace him.

When I write applications, I first design abstract patterns. Those abstract patterns require creativity. Nevertheless, once I publish those patterns, someone else can write a similar application without having to struggle with the design. In other words, someone following can work more efficiently than someone leading can. I really cannot complain because I have followed many brilliant people before me. Their genius propagates itself in others' work, not only in mine, but also in the work of thousands of other people. Their contributions are invaluable because they help many people work more efficiently, but the individual is no longer essential to his ideas. Pressure mounts to keep creating, but what was once genius eventually becomes rote.

Some jobs require less creativity. They require other strengths, for instance, physical agility. As we grow older, we begin to realize that younger people are stronger or more proficient. The harder or longer we work, the less essential we become. We struggle to achieve an edge, but eventually our greatest accomplishment becomes yesterday's trophy. We are walking tragedies. We know that whatever we set out to accomplish, our strength will fall short of the ambition within our hearts. For all our successes, we know we will someday falter and return to dust just as Solomon has said.

Why is man such a broken creature? Paul tells the Romans "All have sinned and fall short of the glory of God."[18] The Apostle Paul does not say we have no glory. He says our glory falls short. Sin obscures our glory. It is less than it is supposed to be. We struggle against our frailty, but eventually our successes become history. Nevertheless, it seems that our failures follow us forever. Our regrets haunt us. This is a symptom of our sin. What is sin that takes the most amazing creature on the planet and reduces him to dust? Where did it begin?

When we look back into Genesis 3, we read about what we call original sin, but is it really the original? In writing to Timothy, Paul gave instructions for the ordination of deacons or overseers. He says that the overseer ". . . must not be a recent convert, or he may become conceited and fall under the

---

[18] Romans 3:23 (NASB)

# The Fall of Man

same judgment as the devil."[19] This verse sounds wildly out of place when referring to people who desire to serve the assembly. Why should a recent convert not have a position of leadership? *Conceit might overtake him.* If he becomes conceited what is the consequence? *He falls under the same judgment as the devil.* This is a serious warning, but it is also enlightening about the nature of the devil. We can infer from this that the devil became conceited and fell under judgment.

Paul's warning makes Ezekiel 28 a little easier to understand. Ezekiel writes:

> The word of the LORD came to me:
> "Son of man, say to the ruler of Tyre,
> 'This is what the Sovereign LORD says:
> "In the pride of your heart
> you say, 'I am a god;
> I sit on the throne of a god
> in the heart of the seas.'"
> But you are a man and not a god,
> though you think you are as wise as a god.'"

God tells the king of Tyre through Ezekiel that he will die a violent death. "Will you then say, 'I am a god,' in the presence of those who kill you?"[20] After this, God again prompts Ezekiel to address the king of Tyre, but this time it appears that Ezekiel is not only addressing the king of Tyre, but also the power behind his throne.

> This is what the Sovereign LORD says:
> "You were the model of perfection,
> full of wisdom and perfect in beauty.
> You were in Eden,
> the garden of God;
> every precious stone adorned you:
> ruby, topaz and emerald,
> chrysolite, onyx and jasper,
> sapphire, turquoise and beryl.
> Your settings and mountings were made of gold;

---

[19] 1 Timothy 3:6 (NIV)
[20] Ezekiel 28:1-2, 9 (NIV)

> on the day you were created they were prepared.
> You were anointed as a guardian cherub,
> for so I ordained you.
> You were on the holy mount of God;
> you walked among the fiery stones.
> You were blameless in your ways
> from the day you were created
> till wickedness was found in you.
> Through your widespread trade
> you were filled with violence,
> and you sinned.
> So I drove you in disgrace from the mount of God,
> and I expelled you, O guardian cherub,
> from among the fiery stones.
> Your heart became proud
> on account of your beauty,
> and you corrupted your wisdom
> because of your splendor.
> So I threw you to the earth;
> I made a spectacle of you before kings.
> By your many sins and dishonest trade
> you have desecrated your sanctuaries.
> So I made a fire come out from you,
> and it consumed you,
> and I reduced you to ashes on the ground
> in the sight of all who were watching.
> All the nations who knew you
> are appalled at you;
> you have come to a horrible end
> and will be no more."[21]

Isaiah chapter 14 gives a similar account of the fall of Satan: God says,

> How art thou fallen from heaven,
> O Lucifer, son of the morning!
> How art thou cut down to the ground,

---

[21] Ezekiel 28:11-19 (NIV)

## The Fall of Man

>Which didst weaken the nations!
>For thou hast said in thine heart,
>"I will ascend into heaven,
>I will exalt my throne above the stars of God:
>I will sit also upon the mount of the congregation,
>in the sides of the north:
>I will ascend above the heights of the clouds;
>I will be like the Most High."
>Yet thou shalt be brought down to hell,
>to the sides of the pit.[22]

John offers yet another view in Revelation, "The great dragon was hurled down – that ancient serpent called the devil, or Satan, who leads the whole world astray. He was hurled to earth, and his angels with him."[23] Jesus says in Luke's Gospel, "I saw Satan fall like lightning from heaven."[24] Although the account of Satan's fall is mentioned only a few times throughout Scripture, we can see both that he was a heavenly being and that he was cast down because of the pride of his heart.

When Ezekiel says of the king of Tyre, "You were in Eden, the garden of God" he does not necessarily mean the Garden of Eden where Adam and Eve were placed, but rather in the paradise of God. We could paraphrase this as, "You were in the paradise of God." This passage refers literally to Satan when he was in the presence of God and figuratively to the human king of Tyre in his luxurious surroundings.

Understanding the fall of Lucifer, or Satan, makes it easier to understand the fall of Adam and Eve in the Garden of Eden. We know that the devil became conceited and then came under judgment. What happened to man, how did he become a fallen creature? First, examine how man and woman came to the garden. The Creator formed Adam from the dust of the ground, but Eve arrived somewhat differently.

>The LORD God said, "It is not good for the man to be alone. I will
>make a helper suitable for him."
>So the LORD God caused the man to fall into a deep sleep; and
>while he was sleeping, he took one of the man's ribs and closed up

---
[22] Isaiah 14:12 – 15 (KJV)
[23] Revelation 12:9 (NIV)
[24] Luke 10:18 (NIV)

# Chapter 2

the place with flesh. Then the LORD God made a woman from the
rib he had taken out of the man, and he brought her to the man.
The man said, "This is now bone of my bones and flesh of my flesh,
she shall be called woman, for she was taken out of the man."[25]

The creation of Eve is intensely personal but distinctively different from Adam's. The Creator did not speak her into existence, nor did he form her from the dust of the ground. He took a rib from Adam's side and formed her from it. Since Adam's rib would have re-grown, he was no less complete for having lost it. Rather from Adam's temporary loss, he gained a partner (Men should remember this in their relationships with their wives). It is also interesting to see that God designed the woman be a helper suitable for Adam.

The man and woman are in the Garden, a special place in all of creation. The Creator comes to the man, interacts with the man, assigns work for the man, and creates a helper for the man and from the man. The Creator is not distant or distracted from the process, but rather he is active and involved. Again this is not smoke, lights, and ethereal music. This Creator looks similar in form to his creation because he created man in his image. The Creator, man, and all creation are in harmony until something awful occurs.

The serpent comes to the woman. We know from Revelation 12 who this serpent really is; from Ezekiel and Isaiah we also know that he has sinned and been cast out of Heaven. The serpent comes to the woman and asks a question, "Did God really say, 'You must not eat from any tree in the garden'?" He knew the answer before asking and he intended to use Eve's answer in arguments against her.

She answers, "We may eat fruit from the trees in the garden, but God did say, 'You must not eat fruit from the tree that is in the middle of the garden, and you must not touch it, or you will die.'"

God did not tell Adam not to touch the tree. Adam might have told Eve, "Don't even touch it. Just leave it alone." Eve may not have been exaggerating the instructions she received. Perhaps Adam added the no-touch rule for her protection.

Nonetheless, the serpent says to the woman, "You will not surely die, For God knows that when you eat of it your eyes will be opened, and you will

---

[25] Genesis 2:18, 21 – 23 (NIV)

## The Fall of Man

be like God, knowing good and evil."[26] This lie, which seduces the woman, recurs often throughout the ages.

Remember the indictment against Satan; he said in his heart, "I shall be like the Most High." Now, after God expelled him from heaven, he is in the Garden of Eden on Earth. Having fallen from his high estate, he encourages Adam and Eve to commit the same sin that caused him to be cast out of heaven. He says, "You will be like God!" *You will be like the Most High!* His lie sets in motion a moral test for man affecting all mankind.

The woman saw that the fruit was good for food. Knowledge appealed to her, so she ate. She gave it also to Adam who was with her, and he ate. Adam and Eve expressed two wrong attitudes. The first was unbelief. The couple chose not to believe the Creator and chose instead to believe a snake. The second attitude was pride. The serpent said, "You will be like God," and it appealed to them.

Lucifer did not think that his position as exalted angel was his proper estate, so he aspired instead to be like the Most High God. In the Garden man usurps what God had not yet given him, specifically the knowledge of good and evil. Man, in a similar way to Lucifer, desired to be like God and overreached his proper position in creation.

Understand and identify this attitude because it is the foundation of false religions and doctrinal heresy. Satan will act as a deceiver, but the heart of man easily aspires to be a god. This deceit, making people think that they are like gods or have no need for God is the work of the devil.

When the king of Tyre said, "I am a god!" Who do you think was whispering in his ear? Nevertheless, his own arrogance brought him down. When the man and woman ate of the tree, their eyes indeed opened, and surprised them by what they saw. Their childlike innocence was shattered. They expected some deeper understanding of *life, the universe, and everything*, but what they realized instead was a little more down to earth: they were naked.

They were naked, exposed, and vulnerable. The Bible says they fastened fig leaves together to cover themselves. It is hard to imagine that the fig leaves worked very well, and so man stumbles forward with his first flawed invention: Fig Leaf Fashion.

---

[26] Genesis 3:1-4 (NIV)

# Chapter 2

After they realize they are naked, and after they try to fashion a covering for themselves, they hear the Creator walking in the garden. Perhaps he did every day, Genesis 3:8 says, "He was walking in the garden in the cool of the day." It almost sounds as if it was customary. They certainly recognized his voice. The Bible does not say, but it sounds like the Creator visiting his creation was a daily event.

When they heard him, the man and woman hid themselves. They thought that perhaps he would become distracted and move on. He did not; instead, the Creator called to the man, "Where are you?" The man replies, "I heard you in the garden, and I was afraid because I was naked; so I hid."[27] Then the man blames the woman, who blames the serpent, but the deed is done and all three bear responsibility. The Creator delivers three curses. The first curse is to the serpent, the second to the woman, and the third to the man.

The curse to the serpent is notable because it says that the offspring from the woman will "crush your head, and you will strike his heel."[28] This is the first promise of Christ's coming.

After cursing the serpent, God turns to the woman, and tells her that her relationships are cursed. She will have pain in childbirth, and her desire will still be to her husband. You may ask, is that part of the curse, really? Yes, remember that God formed the woman to be a suitable helper for man. Just as God designed man to be God's own agent or helper on Earth; God designed woman to be a helper to the man. The desire to fulfill this role will remain, but now God says, "He will rule over you."[29] God is not speaking to Adam here. He is not saying to the man, *you must rule over her*, rather he is telling the woman, *he will do it and you will not like it.*

A paraphrase to Eve might be, *Children and family will cause you great pain. You will seek a normal fulfilling helping relationship with your husband, but it will not work out that way, instead of fulfilling your relationship needs, your husband will rule over you. The relationships that God designed to be thriving and fulfilling will now injure and disappoint you.* Unfortunately, some Christian men do not understand this aspect of the curse, and instead insist that it mandates that they lord over their wives.

---

[27] Genesis 3:8-11 (NIV)
[28] Genesis 3:15 (NIV)
[29] Genesis 3:16 (NIV)

## The Fall of Man

Nevertheless, a husband need not be a tyrant to inflict the curse upon his wife. For example, I work in the yard because I believe its appearance reflects upon me. Lisa does yard work because she loves me. At the end of the day, I am likely to celebrate the appearance of the yard where Lisa would prefer that I acknowledge the sacrifice she made out of love. She feels compelled to fulfill my vision because of our relationship; nevertheless, I might focus upon what we accomplished more than I acknowledge her love. I rule her day without even trying. The satisfaction she seeks is relational, but I still think it was all about the yard. I know this, not because I am so perceptive, but because she told me.

The curse affects woman's relationships to people, and similarly affects man's relationship to the earth. God designed man to have rule over the earth, but now ruling the earth will not be easy. "Cursed is the ground because of you . . . it will produce thorns and thistles for you." To paraphrase: *You will work harder to produce less. You will focus on your job, your dominion and authority. What was supposed to come naturally and gloriously will not reward without disappointment. Success is mitigated by failure.* "By the sweat of your brow you will eat your food until you return to the ground, since from it you were taken; for dust you are and dust you will return."[30] Ultimately, failure will prevail and you will die. The warning given about the *tree of knowledge of good and evil* is true. Hebrews says, "Inasmuch as it is appointed for men to die once . . . after this comes judgment."[31]

Until man dies, he will work. He will strive to gain dominion over the planet. His work will be less fulfilling and less productive than he hopes it will be. In low-light photography, there is a phenomenon called *reciprocity failure*. At low light levels, more photons must actually reach the film or sensor to create an image than are required under normal lighting conditions. Man's career, his dominion, will now experience reciprocity failure. The gains will no longer be proportional to the effort.

Whatever the thorns and thistles we will face, all that makes us great will also make us humble until we eventually die and return to dust. I have never met a man whose vocation did not influence his personal sense of value.

---

[30] Genesis 3:17-19 (NIV)
[31] Hebrews 9:27 (NASB)

# Chapter 2

Winning is everything, but too often we lose. Moreover, a man's conquering instinct will never be fully satisfied from a relationship, nor will a woman's relational instincts ever be fully satisfied in conquest. Because of the curse there is dissonance between the man and the woman.

Robert Frost's poem, *Death of a Hired Man*[viii] is a conversation between a farm couple, Mary and Warren. Silas has returned to their farm with the purpose of working for his board. The poem's most famous line is, "Home is the place where, when you have to go there, they have to take you in." Nevertheless, in the whole of the dialogue, Frost examines the value of a man as it relates to his work: how Silas sees himself, how Warren sees Silas, how Silas sees a college student named Harold. In Silas' mind, the worth of a man condenses down to how he handles the hay with a pitchfork. Warren's view is not much broader; loyalty and perseverance are benchmarks of the man. Harold apparently views education as the key to success, though Silas thinks he can make more of him with a little more time. Each man judges the other based upon his own perceived strengths and the other's apparent weaknesses. For instance, Silas judges Harold based upon Silas' perceived ability to work with a pitchfork, and Warren judges Silas based upon Warren's convictions about loyalty.

After deserting Mary and Warren for higher wages, Silas comes back when he is old and frail. He cannot work anymore, and all he has with which to conjure self-respect are empty promises. Mary, however, sees Silas' value in his relationships; she knows he has nowhere else to go. She understands the fragile pride of a man and has compassion. She feels honored that Silas would choose their humble home for his final hours. The poem reveals the heart of man toward his work and his earth as well as the heart of woman toward her relationships with people. What God ordained is evident even in our art, our creation. Our art tells us that we are frailer than we want to be. We are inadequate and temporary.

Artists, poets, and novelists have often recognized that a man's sense of worth resides in his job, and a woman's sense of worth resides in her relationships. Moreover, men have an intense commitment to the earth, to the ground, to the dirt. God designed man to rule the earth; that much has not changed. Personally the tick infested, thorny, depressed patch of ground in Jamesport means more to me than any other piece of ground on earth. I

# The Fall of Man

spent my weekends and summers there growing up, and it seems that upon those few acres I lived my entire youth. I can understand how men fight wars over rocky, miserable, uninhabitable places. Man came from the ground, and he is still attached to it.

Our hearts cling to the earth because we are from the earth. Paganism says that is all there is, the *Earth*. The earth, Pagans believe, is their mother. By this, they deny accountability to their Creator. Paganism recognizes the connection with the earth, but the earth is not our *mother*. God formed man from the earth by the process of *creation*, not *reproduction*. Likewise, the woman was *created*, not *reproduced*, from the man. Our knowledge of DNA confirms this: a woman's DNA alone cannot produce a man; nevertheless, a man's DNA contains information regarding both genders. Still, a man cannot reproduce without a woman. Therefore, God took Eve out of Adam by the process of creation, not reproduction. Most error begins with a little truth, and even pagans recognize that man came from the earth.

The religion of environmentalism is also a form of paganism. It believes that man exists *for* the earth, but the opposite is true. The earth exists for man (Psalm 8); nevertheless, sin corrupts it, too.

Men's careers and homesteads define them. Many men struggle to make their relationships work, but their hearts lead them down their paths to career success and also to the piece of earth they can call home.

In this modern age, most jobs and careers have less to do with agriculture and the earth. We have insulated ourselves from the earth. Nevertheless, the curse follows a man's career. Work is always harder than it is supposed to be, the yield is usually lower than hoped. There is reciprocity failure. As man transforms himself from dependence on the ground, thorns and thistles morph into competition, regulations, changing requirements, scope creep, and other complications. No technology project is an unmitigated success. In fact, technology projects mitigate otherwise undesirable business realities. Virtual thorns and thistles clog our work environments from country roads to Wall Street.

The curse that God pronounced upon Adam permeates our lives. After years of battling thorns and thistles in various domains, some men retire to the lake, the golf course, the hobby farm, or to some piece of earth where they hope to exert dominion. Billy Bob Thornton performed a hilarious skit on

*Saturday Night Live* about a man and his "fenced-in area." A tiny fenced area behind a trailer home was more important than all his human relationships. The skit was funny because it lampooned a very real human trait. Man seeks to be king of his own domain no matter how small.

Men may move back to the old neighborhood, or to a new neighborhood, or may even take to the open road on a motorcycle or in a motor home. They hope to find the piece of earth, or the experience with earth, that fulfills them. Regardless of what they find or hope to find, eventually they will die leaving all they have accomplished for their heirs and the government to divide.

Henry Wadsworth Longfellow's, *A Psalm of Life* argues that life's meaning is in the struggle and not in the outcome. He differs with Solomon's assessment when he says:

> Tell me not, in mournful numbers,
> Life is but an empty dream! —
> For the soul is dead that slumbers,
> And things are not what they seem.
> Life is real! Life is earnest!
> And the grave is not its goal;
> Dust thou art, to dust returnest,
> Was not spoken of the soul.
> Not enjoyment, and not sorrow,
> Is our destined end or way;
> But to act, that each to-morrow
> Find us farther than to-day.
> Art is long, and Time is fleeting,
> And our hearts, though stout and brave,
> Still, like muffled drums, are beating
> Funeral marches to the grave.
> In the world's broad field of battle,
> In the bivouac of Life,
> Be not like dumb, driven cattle!
> Be a hero in the strife!
> Trust no Future, howe'er pleasant!
> Let the dead Past bury its dead!
> Act, — act in the living Present!

## The Fall of Man

> Heart within, and God o'erhead!
> Lives of great men all remind us
> We can make our lives sublime,
> And, departing, leave behind us
> Footprints on the sands of time;
> Footprints, that perhaps another,
> Sailing o'er life's solemn main,
> A forlorn and shipwrecked brother,
> Seeing, shall take heart again.
> Let us, then, be up and doing,
> With a heart for any fate;
> Still achieving, still pursuing,
> Learn to labor and to wait.[ix]

Despite his inconsistent metaphors, Longfellow is right, "We can make our lives sublime, and departing leave behind us footprints in the sands of time." All life is sublime. However, Longfellow's psalm is hardly the stuff of unmitigated success. "Footprints in the sands of time" sounds fleeting all by itself without even conjuring memories of Shelley's Ozymandius. Longfellow should not have disagreed with Solomon. Longfellow's arguments for enduring glory seems to be *all washed up*.

When we camped at Assateague Island, we left evidence of our every step upon the beach. Nevertheless, the tide cycle erased our footprints and left behind only a pristine beach for whoever was the first to arrive after the tide ran out. While we will always remember Assateague, all evidence of our being there washed away minutes after our departure.

At least Longfellow determines that we are not living for ourselves but for future generations. Nevertheless, we want more, do we not? We want permanence. Solomon knew this, too. He says, "[God] has also set eternity in the hearts of men; yet they cannot fathom what God has done from the beginning to the end."[32] Eternity is the realm of God, and because we are created in his image, we long for it in our hearts. Nevertheless, we cannot grasp God's whole purpose. We cannot because we are human.

What should we expect? The fall of man and the curse we are under leave very little room for mitigation. All we can achieve on this earth becomes

---

[32] Ecclesiastes 3:11 (NIV)

meaningless in death. What we achieve is meaningless except that which we do that pleases God.

Since the fall, man largely tries to do what pleases himself. In Creation God created man in the Creator's image, but since the fall man has largely tried to reverse roles. In the fall, he aspired to be like God, and he has continued the pattern by elevating himself and diminishing his Creator. Since the fall, men have manufactured gods in the image of man or other creatures. Paganism is quick to see the connection to earth, and all too eager to ignore the breath of life from the Creator God. Pagans erect idols, either physical or emotional, that usurp qualities rightfully belonging to God. Paul, preached to the pagans at the Areopagus, sometimes translated *Mars Hill*, and said to them,

> Men of Athens! I see that in every way you are very religious. For as I walked around and looked carefully at your objects of worship, I even found an altar with this inscription: TO AN UNKNOWN GOD. Now what you worship as something unknown I am going to proclaim to you. The God who made the world and everything in it is the Lord of heaven and earth and does not live in temples built by hands.[33]

Paul goes on to proclaim God, the Creator. He says, "In him we live and move and have our being. As some of your own poets have said, 'We are his offspring.'" Paganism might see the connection to the earth. What the Athenians needed to see is their deeper connection and obligation to their Creator. Paul's sermon struck home with some. Even Dionysius a member of the Areopagus was among those who believed. Others could not accept an Almighty God. They could not abandon their pet rocks to find a relationship with their Creator.

Christians, too, sometimes have pet rocks or idols. To the extent that we ascribe frailty to the Most High, we are erecting an idol. We elevate our imagination of God above his true nature. We sometimes find ourselves worshipping God for less than he is; we prefer to worship someone with whom we are more comfortable. When we do this, we are re-creating God in our image.

---

[33] Acts 17:22-24 (NIV)

## The Fall of Man

We went to Mexico with a group of teens several years ago. Cara and Daniel went along, although they were still in elementary school. In the training, I remember one of the youth leaders talking about the need to fellowship with God. She said she imagined God to be an old man, and if she did not pray daily, his poor lonely heart would be broken. What bunk! She was relegating the Creator to a pathetic existence mitigated only by the token compassion of his created. Her self-importance obscured her view of God.

She was like the men of ancient Athens who tended to their garden of the gods, doing for the idols what they could not do themselves. Paul told the Athenians, "[God] is not served by human hands as if he needed anything because he himself gives all men life and breath and everything else."[34] By ascribing neediness to God, she was attempting to ascend above the stars of God. In saying, "God needs me," she was continuing the original sin. The original sin places the creature (or the created) at the center of the universe and displaces, disables, or dismisses the Creator. Within false religions and Christian heresies you will find the common theme. They elevate the creature and diminish the Creator. This is the whisper of the devil, saying, "You will be like God!"

The truth is that we cannot fathom the power of God. Our every imagination falls short. For instance, the Bible says God created the physical universe in six days. Some scientists say otherwise, and so some Christians seek to rationalize. We cannot imagine how God created the entire universe in 144 hours. It is beyond our realm of understanding. Whom we believe is important, however. Are we like God that we can know the origin of the universe? Can we argue with him or with his Word? Through his trials, Job had defended himself against his friends. He tried unsuccessfully to prove his righteousness. God finally spoke to Job saying,

> Where were you when I laid the earth's foundation?
> Tell me, if you understand.
> Who marked off its dimensions?
> Surely you know!
> Who stretched a measuring line across it?
> On what were its footings set,
> Or who laid its cornerstone—

---
[34] Acts 17:25 (NIV)

# Chapter 2

> While the morning stars sang together
> And all the angels shouted for joy?[35]

God continues revealing his power to Job through chapter 41. In Chapter 42, Job answers God.

> I know that you can do all things;
> No plan of yours can be thwarted.
> You ask, 'Who is this that obscures my
> counsel without knowledge?'
> Surely I spoke of things I did not understand,
> Things too wonderful for me to know.
> You said, 'Listen now, and I will speak;
> I will question you, and you shall answer me.'
> My ears had heard of you
> But now my eyes have seen you.
> Therefore I despise myself
> and repent in dust and ashes.[36]

Job was not bad as men go. Before Job's trials, God challenges Satan, saying, "Have you considered my servant Job? There is no one on earth like him; he is blameless and upright, a man who fears God and shuns evil."[37] Throughout the book, Job proclaims his innocence to his friends who wrongfully accuse him. In the end, however, Job repents in dust and ashes, not because he has become any more sinful than in the beginning of the story. He repents because he is a man to whom Creator God has revealed himself.

The Jews were to observe a seven day week, six days of work and a Sabbath of rest, because ". . . in six days the LORD made the heavens and the earth, the sea, and all that is in them, but he rested on the seventh day." Of the Ten Commandments, the fourth commandment is most difficult for Christians to comprehend. We understand "Thou shall not kill", "Thou shall not commit adultery", and "Thou shall not steal." Nevertheless, we stumble over, "Remember the Sabbath." Paul tells us that observance of days is entirely a matter of personal conscience. Does Paul set aside the morality of the fourth commandment?

---

[35] Job 38:4-7 (NIV)
[36] Job 42:2-6 (NIV)
[37] Job 1:8 (NIV)

## The Fall of Man

The moral component of the fourth commandment was never the observance of a day. The proof of this comes by comparison. The second commandment orders Israel not to make any likeness of any creature in heaven or earth; nevertheless, God later commanded Moses to fashion a bronze snake to lift up in the camp. Consequently, the moral component of the second commandment was not the forbidding of making images or likenesses, but forbidding of making objects of worship.

On the seventh day, the Jews were to remember God's six days of creation. While the Law required a day of rest, it was not absolute. It was lawful, for instance, to rescue livestock on the Sabbath day. Male babies were circumcised on the eighth day whether or not it was a Sabbath. The importance of circumcision superseded the importance of resting. Nevertheless, observing the day of rest without remembering creation was a waste of time.

In fact, we learn in Hebrews that the point of the Law was not merely doing things, but rather believing and then acting upon the belief. Of the Israelites who died in the wilderness the writer of Hebrews says, "The message they heard was of no value to them, because those who heard it did not combine it with faith."[38]

The Jews missed the point of the Law and became obsessed with observances without regard to meanings and implications. They observed the Sabbath without fully understanding their obligations to the Creator. That would be similar to my going to work without my laptop. I might spend eight hours at my desk. Nevertheless, without my computer, I am not doing my job.

Some hypothesize that God created the Sabbath to benefit man. This is true, but not in the way they suppose. They propose that six days is enough time to work in a week, and the seventh day of rest is required to refresh and restore the body. While a day of rest is nice, and while our bodies do need refreshing, their hypothesis ignores Scripture's clarity in order to discover their own meaning for the Sabbath. If the Sabbath was designed for man's recreation, then why was man told to rest on the seventh day? Why wouldn't man be told to rest on the most convenient day?

---

[38] Hebrews 4:2 (NIV)

# Chapter 2

Jesus said, "The Sabbath was made for man, not man for the Sabbath."[39] Nevertheless, it was not the commandment to rest that Jesus was emphasizing. In fact, Jesus was trying to say something entirely different. Jesus' disciples were snacking as they walked through a wheat field (this was permissible under the Law). Nevertheless, the Pharisees considered separating the grain from the chaff to be work and the day happened to be a Sabbath. They would have required Jesus' disciples to go hungry rather than do insignificant work in order to eat. Jesus tells them that their opinion was opposite of the truth.

In the context, Jesus was also claiming to be the Creator because he said, "So the Son of Man is Lord even of the Sabbath." *Lord of the Sabbath* equates to *God of Creation* because the Sabbath is inextricably linked to the six-day creation in Exodus 20. To be Lord of the Sabbath and the Son of Man, Jesus would have needed to be the one who initiated the Sabbath as well as the Lord of all men. That is who he claimed to be and that is who he is.

God directed the observance of the day because he wanted Israel to acknowledge him as Creator. That is the only rationale given in Exodus 20:11. A differing opinion is extrabiblical (meaning that it is not found in the Bible). It may be true, but it is not as important as what Scripture says. While man might benefit from rest, man's rest was not God's primary concern. God demanded the Jews to remember weekly that he had created the heavens and the earth in six days and rested on the seventh. Therefore, we are obligated to the moral component of the fourth commandment even if we do not observe the Sabbath day. Paul tells the Colossians,

> Do not let anyone judge you . . . with regard to a religious festival, a New Moon celebration or a Sabbath Day. These are a shadow of things that were to come; the reality, however, is found in Christ.[40]

The New Covenant does not require a weekly observance of a Sabbath day of rest, but God does demand that we acknowledge him as our Creator. Did you notice where Paul says that all the Old Testament observances pointed? Observing the Sabbath is optional; acknowledging the Lord of the Sabbath is required.

---

[39] Mark 2:27, 28 (NIV)
[40] Colossians 2:16-17 (NIV)

# The Fall of Man

Many passages in the New Testament point to Jesus Christ as Creator. Regardless of this, many so-called Christians believe that the *truth* of science informs and corrects Scripture. Science can neither observe nor duplicate what they claim as the origin of life.

Even astronomers peering into deep space at galaxies billions of light years away have no empirical proof to say that the light from those distances actually took billions of years to arrive here. They know how it seems, but they did not trace the light across the expanse of heaven from beginning to end. They know that the speed of light is relative, but they do not know the extent to which that impacts their observations. Moreover, physicists have identified a phenomenon they call *entanglement* wherein quantum systems affect each other across space and time without a traceable means of communication. What if entanglement is common in Creation, would we ever know whether we were seeing the original light from galaxies or merely light from a related quantum system?

I am not pretending to be a scientist; nevertheless, what if our most brilliant astronomers are only a magnitude brighter than Galileo or Copernicus? What if the heavens have not yet revealed one hundredth of a percent of their secrets? Astronomers consequently approach their research with faith in their presuppositions: presuppositions that are based upon and limited by human observation. Someday these assumptions may prove as silly as faith in a flat earth.

An evolutionist bases his beliefs upon his faith in the absence or aloofness of a Creator God, just as a Christian bases his beliefs upon his faith in the existence of a personal Creator God. There is no room for agreement between the two positions. Either God was intimately involved in Creation or he was not. If we do not believe Scripture in this regard, then what *will* we believe from Scripture? If we cannot accept the whole of Scripture, then are we not elevating ourselves above it? If we are elevating ourselves above Scripture, then are we not also elevating ourselves above God whose Word it is? This is binary, true or false, one or zero, all or nothing. Our spiritual understanding is anchored upon the belief that Scripture is the actual Word of God. If we do not believe in its accuracy, we will drift, driven ever further from the truth.

# Chapter 2

    Whatever we think we *know* from science is merely a set of assumptions based upon others' or our own observations. Science still requires faith in these assumptions. Sometimes these assumptions are good enough for now. A scientist can use gravity without understanding it. His hypothesis can be correct within the context of his presuppositions but errant with regard to deeper concepts of which he has no knowledge. Science will never *find* God (although God is the Creator of the physical universe and the universe reflects his glory) because God can only be discovered through the eyes of faith. In fact, we will learn that we do not discover him, but rather he reveals himself. We are advised to place our faith in God and the truthfulness of his Word. Science chases knowledge but faith builds upon the foundation of God's Word.

    A god of evolution is not the God of the Bible. The god of evolution is impersonal and detached, defined by chaos, perhaps even emerging from chaos. Nevertheless, the God of the Bible is personal and intimately involved in his creation. He is a God of order. He is a designer. He is Creator.

    Job always believed in God. Nevertheless, after Job saw God in his power, he repented because of his own weakness and ignorance. We should not try to dummy down our definition of God to suit the world. Our sinful nature greatly hampers our ability to comprehend God's greatness *without* a deliberate attempt to diminish him. The psalmist wrote, "Ascribe strength to God."[41] In fact, the Psalms always sing of God's power.

    If we think that God did not create us as he said he did, then we ascribe our glory to our own innate ability to bring order from chaos. Chaos cannot create order; an infinite number of monkeys cannot duplicate Shakespeare. If we think that we evolved then we also think that we are not accountable to the Creator. In fact, if we think that we evolved, we presume to be the pinnacle of our own creation, and in that lie we embrace the serpent's original deception and pretend to be gods.

    The essence of sin is self-importance. It is self-worship. Sin puffs us up. It makes us think more of ourselves than we should. Sin tells us that we are more important than others are. Sin tells us to please ourselves. Sin convinces us that we do not need God; it says that perhaps God needs us instead.

---

[41] Psalm 68:34 (NASB)

## The Fall of Man

Sin brings death just as God warned Adam in the Garden of Eden. The curse of sin distorts the world in which we live. Woman will strive for fulfilling personal relationships throughout her life. Regardless of her relationships, and sometimes because of them, she will die. Man will strive to conquer the earth, or some small piece of the earth. He will always want his *fenced-in area*. Regardless of his conquests he will die.

A man's career might blossom. There may be times that he is on top of the game, but he will fade. The earth that he was intended to conquer and control will instead conquer him. In time, our bodies will decay into dust. Until then a man will desire to be king and a woman will desire to love and to be loved; neither will be satisfied by the response of the other.

Man's sin corrupted God's great work of Creation. Nevertheless, Creation is not God's greatest work. Paul says, "We know that the whole creation groans and suffers the pains of childbirth together until now."[42] Creation is waiting with us for the completion of God's greatest work.

If we understand God as the Creator, the one who grants us our life and every breath, then we will more easily understand the depths of the mystery of redemption and the New Creation he is bringing about. God is the Almighty Creator who in his wisdom and love formed man from clay and breathed into him the breath of life. Man turned away from God and in so doing incurred the curse that still shapes our very lives and corrupts our world.

---

[42] Romans 8:22 (NASB)

## CHAPTER 3—THE SACRIFICE OF CHRIST

*"Mary and Joseph went to the man at the boss-house and said, 'Boss, do you have any place for Mary to sleep?'*
*"'No.'*
*"Then they went to the other boss and said, 'Do you have any beds for Mary?'*
*"'No.'*
*"And Mary said, 'My baby is about to come out.'*
*"And the boss said, 'You can sleep with my animals.'*
*"But Mary said, 'It's too dirty.' So Mary and Joseph went to the stable, and nothing licked her or bit her, and then Baby Jesus came out!*
*"The animals were so happy, and they loved him. And the angels came, and the shepherds came, and the kings came, and the camels came because they have humps to hold water.*
*"We are so happy that Jesus was born. He is a wonderful baby.*
*"Baby Jesus is the Son of God!"* — Cara age 2 ½

Jesus Christ, the Son of God, the Creator of the universe, became a man, lived a sinless life with all humility, fulfilled the law, and died as a sacrifice for the sins of the entire world. He, who created man, becomes a man, and dies as a sacrifice for man's sin.

There are three perspectives of the Crucifixion of Jesus Christ that we will consider in these pages. What was the sacrifice and why was it necessary? What was our participation in the altar? What does Christ's sacrifice mean in our daily lives?

# Chapter 3

All men, past, present, and future, were present in the Garden of Eden in the person of Adam. In Psalm 139:15, David talks about how God formed him from the earth. David was born of natural parenting, but he visualized himself created in Adam. This is true because God designed each of us, completely and deliberately, at the creation of Adam. Not only did God embed into Adam our potentiality, but he also predestined each one of us. Moreover, this predestination is personal. Zechariah tells us that, "[God] stretches out the heavens, lays the foundation of the earth, and **forms the spirit of man within him**."[43] While our bodies may come about by DNA meandering through the generations from Adam, our spirits share with Adam the Creator's personal attention to detail. Whether we worship God or despise him, our relationship to him is personal. He formed our spirits within us.

Just as all men were present at Creation in Adam, we are also present at Calvary. We are all full legacies of Adam's sin, and therefore we are all spiritually present at the judgment of that sin upon the cross. Hebrews chapter seven supports this reasoning. The writer claims that the Levites tithed to Melchizedek even though they had not yet been born but were still in Abraham's body at the time of the tithe. We need not be physically present in the Garden or at Calvary to be entirely responsible. We are spiritually present at Calvary because it was there that God judged our sin.

All men regardless of the age in which they live carry in them both the sin and the penalty of sin from Adam. Likewise, Paul asserts that believers especially are "participants in the altar." Therefore, whether by inheritance of Adam's sin or by faith in Jesus Christ, all men are present at the crucifixion of Jesus Christ.

**The Sacrifice**

There is a popular notion within Christianity that the process of man's salvation is a battle between good and evil, between God and the devil—the ultimate fight for the souls of men: an *Almighty Smack Down*, coming to a universe near you! Men imagine that with God as their partner, they will tag-team the devil and send him through the ropes and off into the lake of fire. *It is your eternal destiny in the balance, whose side will win?*

---

[43] Zechariah 12:1 (NASB)

## The Sacrifice of Christ

This fiction also promotes parallel fictions such as the *kingdom of hell* or the *power of hell* as rivals to the kingdom of God and his power. These concepts are not in the Bible; moreover, they are unbiblical. Only once in the whole Bible do *hell* and *power* appear together in the same verse. Hades, or Hell, follows one of the Four Horsemen of the Apocalypse, named Death. *Death*, is given authority, or power, to kill one fourth of the earth's population. Nevertheless, who gives Death such authority? *From Revelation 6:7-8, it is obvious that the Lamb gives him authority: the resurrected, glorified Jesus Christ gives authority to Death!*

God has delegated to them all the power Death and Hell have upon this earth. Still myths persist within various churches that summarize redemption as a struggle between good and evil, a pitched battle between God and the devil for the souls of men.

Such silliness is reinforced by allegorical readings of C. S. Lewis' *The Lion, the Witch, and the Wardrobe*.[x] Edmond is under a magical curse and is in bondage to the white witch until Aslan redeems Edmund from the witch. Aslan accomplishes this by submitting to his own execution on the stone table. Alas, the tables are turned, and after the witch is satisfied, Aslan's deeper magic resurrects him from the dead, and the final battle ensues. Aslan redeems Edmund, the witch is defeated, and Narnia is freed. It is a nice story, but it is not the Gospel story. The deal-with-the-devil idea also crops up in Christian entertainment and music. People sing and speak as if the devil must be bargained with, defeated, or at least outwitted before God can save men's souls.

The Gospels Matthew, Mark, and Luke record Jesus talking about binding the "strong man" and "plundering his house." Some people mistakenly apply this as an allegory for redemption. They believe that Jesus bound Satan at the cross to steal back the souls of men. Nevertheless, this is not what Jesus was teaching. Jesus was claiming that he has authority over Satan anytime, anywhere. Power over Satan is not something that Jesus will gain; it is something that he has always held! In the context of the story, Jesus has just delivered a man from demonic possession. Jesus tells the Jews that he could not have done this unless he was more powerful than the devil.

Satan was defeated the instant evil was found in his heart. At that moment, God expelled him from heaven, and from that moment, he was

# Chapter 3

under the eternal judgment of God. John writes, "The one who practices sin is of the devil; for the devil has sinned from the beginning. The Son of God appeared for this purpose, to destroy the works of the devil."[44] After falling due to pride, Satan tried to assert his importance once again into the affairs of men. The Son of God destroyed Satan's work, however, when sin no longer had a grip on man. Genesis chapter 3 tells us that the serpent will bruise the Savior's heel, but the Savior will crush the serpent's head. This figurative comparison is proportional: Satan's impact is minimal, but Christ destroys him. Christ destroys Satan without directly engaging him in a struggle. Hebrews says Jesus destroyed the devil at the cross.

> Since the children have flesh and blood, [Jesus] shared in their humanity **so that by his death he might destroy** him who holds the power of death—that is, **the devil**—and free those who all their lives were held in slavery by their fear of death.[45]

A closer look at this verse and we learn two things about the devil that are vitally important to correct doctrine. First, the devil holds the power of death. Secondly, the *power of death* that he holds is actually man's *fear of death*. How does Satan hold man by the power of the fear of death? *He deceives man,* causing him, in light of his mortality, to pursue self-gratification and self-justification (*La vie Bohème*, for example) rather than pursuing forgiveness and reconciliation from his Creator.

Self-justification also includes religious *third-party endorsements* such as baptism, church membership, initiations, penitence, or other external standards by which people assure themselves of salvation. Jesus says, "Many will say to Me on that day, 'Lord, Lord, did we not prophesy in your name, and in your name perform many miracles?'" To these who seek to justify themselves, Jesus says, "I never knew you; DEPART FROM ME."[46] Those who hope in anything other than the blood of Jesus Christ are deceived. In their deception, their fear of death compels them to seek justification by means other than what God has provided with the sacrifice of Christ. Darkness holds men, not by brute force, but by deceit.

Consequently, destruction of the devil's power does not imply a battle, a divine deception, or a negotiation for the souls of men. With the sacrifice of

---

[44] 1 John 3:8 (NASB)
[45] Hebrews 2:14 (NIV)
[46] Matthew 7:22, 23 (NASB)

## The Sacrifice of Christ

Jesus' blood, mankind was reconciled to God. Satan was defeated. Redeemed man must no longer fear death. John's statement, "the one who practices sin is of the devil," can confuse us; nevertheless, sinners are of the devil because they are still deceived by the devil. Their *fear of death* still controls them. Prior to death, religion and philosophy promote self-justification, self-gratification, or both; these are the works of the devil that are destroyed by the Gospel of salvation by grace through faith.

John says that Jesus Christ appeared to destroy the works of the devil. The works of the devil are to steal, kill, and destroy. The devil's weapon is deception; and Jesus' truth destroys Satan's lies. At salvation, we no longer have a fear of death, and Satan is subsequently powerless over us. Satan's defeat comes by Jesus Christ reconciling man unto his Creator.

When Paul preached to Agrippa in Acts 26, he quoted Jesus saying that men "[turn] from the dominion of Satan to God."[47] This is one of few Scriptures referencing the *dominion* or *kingdom* of Satan. Jesus says elsewhere that a kingdom divided cannot stand; nevertheless, he was speaking hypothetically. Moreover, in that circumstance he was asserting that his authority came from God, *not* that Satan had a kingdom. His intent was not to inform us about the *kingdom of Satan*; consequently, we should not infer anything specific about the devil's kingdom. Oblique references alone do not provide deep insight. Furthermore, our inferences are speculation, hearsay, or mythology, none of which is valuable to the believer. In Acts 26, there are not concrete political analogies. Therefore, a better word choice for the translators would have been *domination*. Domination communicates power over men without implying political hierarchy.

Consequently, God facilitated men's turning from Satan's domination unto himself, Jesus says, by God's opening men's eyes. It had everything to do with God revealing the truth to man and man responding to the truth. The truth overcame the deceit. God did not bargain with, double-cross, or battle with the devil. Rather God opened the eyes of the blind!

Surely, Satan would snatch this truth away as Jesus also described in Matthew 13, but our salvation does not depend upon the devil—not his power and not his demise—rather our salvation depends on how God draws us and how we respond to him. Paul tells the Colossians that God forgave our sins,

---
[47] Acts 26:18 (NASB)

# Chapter 3

"having canceled out the certificate of debt consisting of decrees against us . . . and He has taken it out of the way, having nailed it to the cross."[48] Our sin offended God, and it was to him we owed a debt. Jesus Christ, the God-Man, paid our debt with his *human* body and blood.

Jesus did not destroy sin in a battle against the devil as C. S. Lewis' allegory paints; he destroyed sin, which is disobedience toward God, through total obedience to his Father. By destroying sin, he destroyed the penalty of sin, which is death. Paul says, "Death has been swallowed up in victory."[49] While Satan can exercise the fear of death to enslave men, death is the righteous judgment of God!

Since God pronounced death as the penalty for sin, man is not under the judgment of the devil. God did not say to Eve, "The devil will greatly increase your pains." He said, "I will greatly increase your pains." Mankind is under the judgment of God! God said, "When you eat of it you will surely die." Remember Solomon says, "God will bring every deed into judgment, including every hidden thing, whether it is good or evil." Satan is the imposter, the deceiver. An imposter positions himself as the real thing. He is gratified when he deceives. Satan would probably like us to think that he has something to say about our salvation. Satan would deceive people to think their salvation was dependent upon him in order to elevate himself and detract from the work of God.

This false concept of the devil is apparent in many Charismatic churches, especially in their prayers. When some pray, they are in one breath praying to God and in the next breath praying to the devil. While they say good stuff to God and bad stuff to the devil, they glorify the devil by giving him standing in their prayers. It is as if they worship two gods. They ignore Jude's warning. Jude says of those who blaspheme the devil, "These men speak abusively against whatever they do not understand; and what things they do not understand by instinct, like unreasoning animals—these are the very things that destroy them."[50] In other words, the men who speak abusively of the devil, the devil will destroy. Jude goes on to use strong language including the words "twice dead" to describe such men.

---

[48] Colossians 2:14 (NASB)
[49] 1 Corinthians 15:54 (NIV)
[50] Jude 10 (NIV)

## The Sacrifice of Christ

The word translated *speak abusively* in Jude 10 actually transliterates to "blaspheme" in English. We visited a church once where the pastor's wife was teaching the elementary children how to *battle* the devil. What she was actually teaching them was to blaspheme the devil. What is wrong with that? *We are to show God the respect that is due him by understanding our position with regard to his authority over the whole creation. Satan was once a guardian cherub, who are we to speak abusively to him?*

Jude uses Michael, the archangel, as a positive example of how to handle a confrontation with the devil. He writes, "Even the archangel Michael, when he was disputing with the devil about the body of Moses, did not dare to bring a slanderous accusation against him, but said, 'The Lord rebuke you!'"[51] The Old Testament prophet Daniel describes Michael as "the great prince who stands guard over [Israel]."[52] If anyone had authority to level accusations at the devil, you would think it would be Michael. Michael, the guardian of Israel, with his trumpet will someday announce the Lord's return.

Nevertheless, Michael understands that the devil is only powerful if we allow him to deceive, so he says, "The Lord rebuke you." Remember that at the devil's own downfall he was elevating his own importance. He is still active trying to deceive men regarding his power and relevance.

James, Jude's brother, says, "Submit yourselves, then, to God. Resist the devil, and he will flee from you."[53] James makes it clear that what is important is our relationship to God. The devil is relevant only because he seeks to destroy us by his deceit. We have to cooperate with him in order for him to have influence in our lives, just as Adam and Eve had to cooperate in their own deception when they rebelled against God. The devil is powerless if we obey God and resist deception.

Moreover, man does not need to be redeemed from the devil. Christ *delivers* men from bondage caused by the fear of death, but he *redeems* them from God's righteous judgment. The former is an indirect consequence, while the latter is God's glorious work of salvation. The process of the redemption must satisfy God alone because it was his law that man disobeyed. Paul

---

[51] Jude 9 (NIV)
[52] Daniel 12:1 (NASB)
[53] James 4:7 (NIV)

writes, "The wrath of God will come upon the sons of disobedience."[54] Notice that it is the wrath of God which comes upon the disobedient, not the wrath of Satan. Hebrews gives a precise account of the sacrifice of Jesus Christ. The writer says, "The blood of Christ, who through the eternal Spirit offered himself unblemished to God, [will] cleanse our consciences." There is no devil in the redemption details.

In Matthew 4:1-11, the devil tempts Jesus. The devil offers him all the kingdoms of the world in exchange for credit the devil thought was his due, but Jesus would not bargain with the devil for the souls of men. Remember God did not deal with the devil for Adam and Eve. Rather he told the serpent that the seed or offspring of the woman would crush the serpent's head. Jesus did not negotiate with the devil in the desert. He did not and he never will. Jesus' death, and the redemption of mankind, has restored all that Satan sought to destroy. Now man can again have a proper relationship with God.

After Adam and Eve sinned, God replaced the fashion fad of fig leaves with animal skin. Immediately after man sinned the Creator began mitigating the affects of sin. He covers Adam and Eve's nakedness better than they alone could do. He sends them out of the Garden so that they cannot eat of the Tree of Life and consequently live forever in their fallen state. God punishes them in such a way that makes redemption possible.

God initiates blood sacrifice with the animal skin he used as a covering for Adam's sin. At the next sacrifice mentioned in Genesis, Abel offered fat portions from some of the firstborn of his flock. There was no need for Abel to light the fire. The Lord in the person of the Son was present to receive the offerings of Cain and Abel. Perhaps Abel saw fire come down from heaven to consume his offering as Gideon also witnessed in Judges 6:21 and as Elijah did in 1 Kings 18. Nevertheless, Abel's offering was acceptable but Cain's offering of vegetables was not. Abel's act of worship was a face-to-face meeting with the Creator.

Jehovah God met face to face with men numerous times in the Old Testament including Gideon's offering of a goat, bread, and broth. Cain and Abel brought their offerings to God, a pre-incarnate appearance of Christ.

Noah offered sacrifices of burnt offerings immediately following the flood. This was the first time that the Bible mentions burnt offerings. They

---

[54] Colossians 3: 6 (NASB)

## The Sacrifice of Christ

may have existed before the flood; nevertheless, this is the first mention of them. Abraham and the patriarchs of Israel offered burnt offerings to the Lord. Job offered burnt offerings on behalf of his children, in case they might have sinned and cursed God in their hearts.

The Law of Moses formalized rules regarding tabernacle and temple sacrifices performed by the Levites, but burnt offerings and fellowship offerings also occurred outside of temple or tabernacle worship. King David, after sinning by taking a census of his fighting men (an act contrary to faith in God), buys a threshing floor, builds an altar, and offers burnt offerings and fellowship offerings. The plague that was afflicting the land ended then in answer to David's prayer.

The book of Hebrews makes it clear that no real atonement occurs in the Old Testament sacrifices. The sacrifices were recurring and they "were not able to clear the conscience of the worshiper."[55] Still Hebrews explains: "The law requires that nearly everything be cleansed with blood, and without the shedding of blood there is no forgiveness."[56] Nevertheless, the sacrifices expressed the faith of the worshiper. "By faith Abel offered God a better sacrifice than Cain did. By faith he was commended as a righteous man, when God spoke well of his offerings."[57]

While the sacrifices of the Old Testament were proper and necessary, they did not earn redemption or the forgiveness of sin. They pointed forward to the once-for-all sacrifice of Jesus Christ, and they proved the faith of the worshiper. Of the several sacrifices sanctioned in Leviticus, two in particular stand out as types, or symbols, of Jesus Christ: the *Passover* and the sin offering on the *Day of Atonement*. Likewise, the *Lord's Supper* from the New Testament looks back at Christ's sacrifice, and forward to his coming again. The Passover pictures Christ's atoning sacrifice from man's perspective on earth. The Day of Atonement pictures Christ's atoning sacrifice as it deals with sin; it includes the perspective of God's mercy seat in heaven. The Lord's Supper pictures Christ's sacrifice as it is manifest in our daily lives.

---

[55] Hebrews 9:9 (NIV)
[56] Hebrews 9:22 (NIV)
[57] Hebrews 11:4 (NIV)

## Chapter 3

**The Passover**

The Passover celebrates an historical event. The children of Israel had been in Egypt for 430 years. Initially they were welcomed. Joseph, son of Israel (Jacob), had become a ruler in Egypt. The entire clan moved to Egypt during a famine. Joseph, himself, was a type of Christ. His brothers conspired against him and sold him into slavery. God intervened eventually and made him a governor of Egypt. His exalted position was the salvation of the whole family. In the same manner, the Crucifixion, where man conspired to do evil, was God's provision of eternal life for those who believe.

Nevertheless, after 430 years of Israel's descending into slavery, God sent Moses to confront Pharaoh and secure the release of the Israelites. Pharaoh was not cooperative and God sent a series of plagues upon Egypt. Each plague discredited an Egyptian deity. Pharaoh was repeatedly unconvinced until the first Passover. On the Passover, God told Israel to kill a lamb, paint its blood on the top and sides of the doorframe. Each family was to prepare the lamb over the fire, they were to eat unleavened bread, or bread without yeast. They were to cook the lamb in one piece; no bone was to be broken. They were to consume the whole lamb; and whatever they did not eat, they were to burn completely before morning. They were to eat the meal with urgency. Each person was to have his sandals on and his robe tucked in: ready to leave quickly. Even though the Seder has come to be an evening of leisure, it was originally a night of readiness and anticipation.

At midnight on Passover, God killed the firstborn of every family in Egypt: from the poorest family to Pharaoh's own firstborn. The angel of death even killed the firstborn among the livestock. Nevertheless, within the houses with the blood on the door, no one died. The angel passed over those houses, and all within them were safe, but as for the houses without the blood, "There was loud wailing in Egypt, for there was not a house without someone dead."[58]

God commanded that Israel observe the Passover forever. God also commanded Israel to observe the Sabbath forever, and we will discuss the relevance of that a little later. Nevertheless, the Passover was the only feast that was ordained forever. Not coincidentally, the Last Supper of Jesus and his disciples was a Passover celebration. We know that it was Passover

---

[58] Exodus 12:30 (NIV)

# The Sacrifice of Christ

because Jesus said to his disciples while they were reclining at the table, "I have eagerly desired to eat this Passover with you before I suffer."[59] Some argue that the Last Supper was not a Passover celebration, but a graduation party for the disciples. They argue that Jesus could not have celebrated a Passover meal a day early. Nevertheless, a brief study reveals that Jesus celebrated the Passover with his disciples and died as the Passover Lamb the following day. While this sounds contradictory, there is no conflict in the Gospel accounts.

In the year of Jesus' crucifixion, Passover would have occurred on Thursday, the day of Jesus' crucifixion. We can know the Crucifixion occurred on Thursday and not Friday, as most churches celebrate, because Jesus said, "The Son of Man [will] be three days and three nights in the heart of the earth."[60] The Jews also demanded a Roman guard at Jesus tomb for three days, lest his disciples steal Jesus' body and claim a resurrection. Jesus rose from the dead on the first day of the week, or Sunday, after "three days and three nights" in the grave. Do the math, and always believe Scripture above even millennia of church tradition.

Jesus was crucified on Thursday; nevertheless, Mark says that Jesus celebrated the Passover with his disciples in the evening on the day that the lambs were slaughtered. John's Gospel says that Jesus died on the day of preparation for the Passover. There seems to be a disagreement in the Scriptural record. Nevertheless, the apparent disagreement concerns how each writer calculated the days and by what each writer meant by the word *Passover*.

The word *Passover* can mean: the week of the feast, the day of the sacrifice, and the Passover meal. Likewise, we might talk about Christmas and mean the season, a school vacation, the day of Christmas, or a gift exchange. We determine the actual meaning from the context of our reference. Cara might say that she wants to come home for Christmas, which means she intends to travel during her break from school. Claire, on the other hand might be more interested in what present she will be getting on Christmas morning. Daniel might refer to Christmas meaning the retail-shopping season beginning around Thanksgiving and ending at New Years

---

[59] Luke 22:15 (NIV)
[60] Matthew 12:40 (NASB)

## Chapter 3

Eve. We all might use the same word in different contexts at different times to mean different things, but we would think people were silly if they thought we meant that Christmas Day was anything other than December 25.

The timing of Passover, however, is more complex because of the three calendars used at the time of Christ. One calendar, called the Diaspora, calculated days beginning in the morning. The traditional Jewish calendar calculated days beginning in the evening. The Roman, Julian calendar, from which we derive our calendar system calculated the days beginning at midnight.

According to the Diaspora, the Passover that year began on Wednesday at dawn. Jews observing this calendar ate the Passover lamb on the same calendar day as the sacrifice, or Wednesday evening. According to the Diaspora calendar, both the Passover preparation and the Passover meal were observed on Wednesday. However, according to the evening calendar they probably would not have sacrificed lambs until Thursday morning. John refers to the day of crucifixion as the day of "preparation for the Passover" and the day of "preparation for the Sabbath." According to the evening calendar, the day of preparation for the Passover (the day of sacrifice) occurred *between the twilights* of Wednesday and Thursday. The lamb was sacrificed during the day and eaten in the evening after a *new* day, the special Passover Sabbath (and the Feast of Unleavened Bread), had begun. This special Sabbath day lasted until twilight Friday when the regular Sabbath began. Jesus rose from the dead sometime after the Sabbath ended, and he was first seen by Mary Magdalene on Sunday morning.

In this way, Jesus could celebrate the Passover on Wednesday, and could still be the Passover Lamb on Thursday. Joseph and Nicodemus would have buried Jesus early Thursday evening before twilight while it was still the *day of preparation* for the Passover *meal*. John discusses the urgency with which they buried him because it was still the day of preparation.

Matthew, Mark, and Luke write from the perspective of the Diaspora calendar, but John writes from the perspective of the traditional calendar regarding Jewish ceremony but according to the Roman calendar otherwise. Jesus calculated the date of his Passover sacrifice according to the traditional calendar, as well. The calendar that each writer references, is revealed by how they calculated the hours of the day or how they described the timing of

# The Sacrifice of Christ

events. With this understanding, the various Gospel accounts meld together in a coherent narrative of the Passion Week.

On the Sunday preceding the Passover, the 10th day of the month, the lamb was to be chosen and set aside. This was the day Jesus entered Jerusalem and began teaching in the temple courts. Luke says of this week, "Every day he was teaching in the temple."[61] Jesus was there in the temple that week because he was the chosen Passover sacrifice. The Lamb was set aside at the appropriate time. Jesus, the Lamb, was observed for the four days that were required.

The following Wednesday evening Jesus brought his disciples together to celebrate the Passover. It was at this, the Passover-Last Supper, that Jesus "took bread, gave thanks, and broke it, and gave it to his disciples, saying, 'Take and eat; this is my body.'" He then took the cup of wine and said, "Drink from it, all of you. This is the blood of the covenant, which is poured out for many for the forgiveness of sins."[62]

Paul calls Jesus "our Passover" and then tells the Corinthians to celebrate the feast "with the unleavened bread of sincerity and truth."[63] Jesus is our Passover Lamb, and our Passover celebration is the feast of the Lord's Supper. Remember that Israel was to celebrate the Passover forever, and now God prescribes the Passover for the church, albeit with changes in practice. Whereas the Passover required a sacrificial lamb, Jesus, our Passover, has been sacrificed once for all. The Jews celebrated Passover annually, but the New Testament tradition celebrated Jesus as the Passover Lamb each week on Sunday. We will discuss this again later.

The Passover pictures for us the promise of the sacrifice of Jesus Christ and our subsequent deliverance from the bondage of sin. The Lord's Supper frames the same picture albeit from the perspective of Christ's completed work. Nevertheless, before more discussion of the Lord's Supper, we will first consider some other dimensions of the sacrifice of Christ.

**The Day of Atonement**

During the Sin Offering described in Leviticus 4, the high priest sprinkled blood in front of the curtain inside the temple or tabernacle, he

---

[61] Luke 19:47 (NIV)
[62] Matthew 26:26-28 (NIV)
[63] 1 Corinthians 5:8 (NASB)

## Chapter 3

spread it on the horns of the altars, and then poured the rest out in front of the altar of the burnt offering. On the Day of Atonement, the high priest sprinkled blood behind the curtain of the Most Holy Place in front of the atonement cover. This could occur only once a year, and only the high priest could bring the blood into the Most Holy Place. Any other time, or any other person, and the result would be death. In addition, before the priest could offer blood for the atonement of the people's sin, he had to first offer a blood sacrifice for himself.

The writer of Hebrews makes it clear that Jesus as the supreme high priest offered his own blood in the Most Holy Place, that is not the earthly temple or tabernacle, but in the very presence of God the Father. The descriptions of the Day of Atonement differ from the Passover because it includes a picture of Christ's sacrifice before God in heaven in addition to his sacrifice here on earth. The writer of Hebrews celebrates the superiority of Christ's sacrifice over the sacrifice of goats and bulls,

> How much more, then, will the blood of Christ, who through the eternal Spirit offered himself unblemished to God, cleanse our consciences from acts that lead to death, so that we may serve the living God![64]

The sacrifice of Jesus Christ fulfills the requirements of the Law once for all. "But now he has appeared once for all at the end of the ages to do away with sin by the sacrifice of himself."[65]

In the sacrifice of Jesus Christ pictured by the Day of Atonement, he is both the high priest and sin offering. He offers himself, through the Holy Spirit, to God the Father. Isaiah 53 offers additional prophetic insight: "It was the LORD's will to crush him and cause him to suffer."[66] The sacrifice of Jesus Christ was ordained by God the Father, offered in obedience by the Son, and effected through the Holy Spirit. Jesus was not a *victim* of a crucifixion, but rather an obedient and willing sacrifice. In Romans, Paul contrasts Adam's disobedience to Jesus' obedience:

> For just as through the disobedience of one man the many were made sinners, so also through the obedience of the one man the many will be made righteous . . . just as sin reigned in death, so also

---

[64] Hebrews 9:14(NIV)
[65] Hebrews 9:26b (NIV)
[66] Isaiah 53:10 (NIV)

## The Sacrifice of Christ

grace might reign through righteousness to bring eternal life through Jesus Christ our Lord.[67]

Therefore, all members of the Godhead were involved in redemption in much the same way they were all involved in creation. God the Father ordained and approved the sacrifice of Jesus Christ. The blood of Christ was offered through the "eternal Spirit." This statement, *through the eternal Spirit*, dispels a myth that says that Jesus was totally cut off from God.

While Jesus was cut off from the Father, his sacrifice was made *through* the Spirit. Jesus in his humanity felt isolated by the weight of the sins of the world, and cried out, "My God, My God, Why have you forsaken me?" Nevertheless, it was by the power of God in the Holy Spirit that he was able to complete the sacrifice for sin. Jesus' sacrifice, carried into the Most Holy Place in the presence of the Father, restored the fellowship that our sin had interrupted.

In the Old Testament God accepted animal sacrifices as acts of faith for the forgiveness of sin. We know they had no permanent effect, but they pointed forward to Jesus Christ. While it is somewhat easy to see that the Old Testament sacrifices pointed forward to Jesus Christ and his death, it may be more difficult to understand the reason for the sacrifice, why God required it, and what the sacrifice of his Son accomplished.

One episode from the Old Testament is especially relevant to our discussion because it pictures for us the meaning of Christ's sacrifice. When the children of Israel are in the wilderness between Egypt and the Promised Land, recorded in Numbers 21, the people complained against God and Moses. Consequently, God sent poisonous snakes into the camp and many died as a result. The snakes reminded Israel of Adam's rebellion and the penalty of sin.

The people then came to Moses to confess their sin and asked Moses to pray that God would take away the snakes. Moses prayed, but God did not take away the snakes, at least not immediately. Instead, God had Moses fashion a bronze snake and put it on a pole that was lifted up in the camp where it could be seen. When a snake bit someone, he could look to the snake on the pole for healing.

---

[67] Romans 5:19 – 20 (NIV)

# Chapter 3

Now this is a curious situation. God forbade the children of Israel from making idols, yet here God commands Moses to fashion a snake (Centuries later King Hezekiah destroyed Moses' bronze snake because people were burning incense to it. Read about it in 2 Kings 18:4). Moses made the snake from bronze. Bronze in Scripture is a symbol of judgment; and the snake symbolizes sin. Together they symbolize the judgment of sin. So the question is what was in God's mind, that he would command Moses to create an object that would eventually become an idol to the people? What was so important about the bronze snake? Why didn't God just drive the snakes away? Jesus answers that question:

> Just as Moses lifted up the snake in the desert, so the Son of Man must be lifted up, that everyone who believes in him may have eternal life. For God so loved the world that he gave his one and only Son that whoever believes in him shall not perish, but have eternal life.[68]

Moses' serpent is a type or foreshadowing of Jesus Christ on the cross. All who looked to the snake lived, and all who look to the work of Christ on the cross are saved. Looking to the snake required an act of faith on the part of the afflicted person. Likewise, a sinner must look to the work on the cross in faith and believe.

That still does not explain why Moses put a bronze snake on a pole. Why a snake? Why not a bull, goat, or lamb, some type of *clean* sacrificial animal? Nevertheless, Moses' serpent was not a typical symbol of Christ, but rather it was a symbol for the judgment of sin. Paul clarifies the imagery when he writes, "God made him who had no sin to be sin for us, so that in him we might become the righteousness of God."[69] Moses' serpent then is not a picture of a holy, sinless, Christ, but a Christ who has taken on the sin of the world and the accompanying judgment!

Moses' serpent is not the only picture of Christ becoming sin. On the Day of Atonement, two goats were selected. One was sacrificed for the sins of the people. Its blood was sprinkled on the mercy seat. The other, the scapegoat, was taken outside the camp into the wilderness. Before the goat was led away, the high priest would put his hands on the goat's head

---

[68] John 3:14-16 (NIV)
[69] 2 Corinthians 5:21 (NIV)

# The Sacrifice of Christ

symbolically transferring the sin of the people to the sacrifice. The scapegoat symbolically became the sin of the nation of Israel, just as Jesus in reality became our sin on the cross outside the gates of the city Jerusalem. The symbolism of the two goats pictures one sacrifice in two dimensions. Before the scapegoat could bear the sins of Israel, the blood of the sin offering had to find approval at the mercy seat. Likewise, the dimensions of Jesus' sacrifice include his worthiness before God and his carrying the sins of the world into judgment.

God judged sin on the cross by the death of Jesus Christ. Jesus, the innocent, became sin and endured the judgment of sin, which is death. Therefore, we become the righteousness of God by believing in Jesus Christ, the Son of God. Just as God spared the Israelites from death by snakebite when they looked to the bronze serpent on the pole, God saves us from the penalty of sin when we look to Christ who became our sin upon the cross. What a contrast! Jesus, the sinless, becomes sin, and man the sinner, becomes the righteousness of God.

## The Lord's Supper

At the Passover Last Supper, Jesus initiated the ordinance the church calls *Communion*: the bread and the wine. Instead of *Communion*, we should call this event the *Lord's Supper* or the *Eucharist*. Eucharist is a transliteration from the Greek word meaning *I give thanks*. Eucharist encapsulates the meaning of the command better than the word, *Communion*. Likewise, the term *Lord's Supper* also conveys meaning better than *Communion* does. *Eucharist* recalls that after Jesus gave thanks that he broke the bread. The *Lord's Supper* recalls that we eat his supper for his remembrance.

We will see later that there are communal aspects of the Lord's Supper; nevertheless, because the Bible does not refer to it as *Communion*, there are better names for us to use. The term *Lord's Supper* is biblical and *Eucharist* at least remembers Jesus' words, albeit obliquely. If someone were to ask what we meant by *Lord's Supper* or *Eucharist* we could explain the meaning from a scriptural context. *Communion*, on the other hand, is a name containing only the meaning we assign to it. Historically it has indicated a relationship to a church organization (Anglican Communion, for instance) rather than a relationship to Christ; consequently, it obfuscates truth rather than communicating it.

The Lord's Supper has its foundation in the Passover feast and its memory should not be divorced from our understanding of the Lord's Supper. At this Last Passover Supper, Jesus revised the celebration; specifically he elevated the importance of the unleavened bread and the wine. Because Jesus is the Passover sacrifice, there remains no need to continue sacrificing a lamb and painting blood on the door frames. We still remember that Jesus Christ is our Passover and we celebrate with the bread and wine. The menu and the schedule change, but the central idea remains.

Instead of celebrating once a year at Passover we are now to celebrate often or whenever we can. The early church celebrated the Lord's Supper weekly. The Mosaic Law looked forward to Christ as the Passover Lamb. The Lord's Supper institutes the New Covenant, which looks back to Christ's sacrificial death as our Passover Lamb and forward to his return and the Marriage Supper of the Lamb.

In the New Covenant, we do not observe seasons and their various celebrations (at least not by Scriptural command), but rather we have one celebration that we celebrate all the time. Hebrews 4 tells us that we are given a special day to commemorate. God commanded Israel to commemorate the Sabbath forever, but our special day is *Today*. This hints at the difference between the ritual religion of the Old Covenant and the New Covenant relationship between God and man.

There is not *one* day in each week, or month, or year that is special to a Christian because *Today* (everyday) is a special and appropriate day to respond to God in worship. Moreover, our Passover lamb is no longer from a flock of sheep. Rather our Passover Lamb is Jesus Christ, and our Passover celebration is no longer a Seder held once a year each spring according to the phases of the moon, but rather the Lord's Supper that we celebrate as often as we do. The calendar does not dictate the form of our worship, but rather our expressions of worship are freely given. Actually, the Sabbath and the Passover, which God commanded Israel to observe forever, are still observed by the church. Nevertheless, our celebrations are without regard to the calendar because *Today* is our special day and our Passover feast is the Lord's Supper.

# The Sacrifice of Christ

When we celebrate the Lord's Supper, we do not celebrate an exodus from Egypt, but rather we celebrate our escape from the bondage of sin by the body and blood of Jesus Christ. The Exodus from Egypt was a type or foreshadowing of the truth that Christ accomplished as our Passover. In that sense the Old Testament celebration of the Passover and the Eucharist are the same. They both look to the sacrifice of Jesus Christ on the cross.

Even the symbolism of the Passover foretells the cross. When we view in our mind's eye the blood on the wooden lintel and doorposts, we can overlay the bloodstains from Jesus' head and hands upon the cross. The bloodstained cross now becomes our refuge just as the bloodstained doorways opened for Israel a safe haven from the angel of death. Likewise, the Lord's Supper looks back to the cross at the body and blood of the Lord Jesus Christ.

The nature of the elements chosen to celebrate this feast is revealing. The Passover bread was unleavened, without yeast. The Old Testament Law forbids yeast anywhere within the country during the week of Passover. At the original Passover, the Bible says that they carried their bread dough out of their homes without yeast because Israel left Egypt in haste; they did not have time to add yeast. While the unleavened bread reminds the Jews of the urgency with which they fled Egypt, it conveys even deeper significance to Christians.

In the New Testament, leaven is always a symbol of sin. Some theologians exempt Matthew 13 and Luke 13 from this, but when they do, they fail to understand what Jesus was really saying. Elsewhere, Jesus warns people, "Be on guard against the yeast of the Pharisees which is hypocrisy."[70] What is hypocrisy? *It is inconsistency between what we say or think we are and what we truly are.* It is prideful and arrogant. It thinks better of itself than it should. Likewise, leaven puffs up. In Matthew 16:11 Jesus compares yeast to the teaching of the Pharisees and Sadducees—again yeast is arrogance, self-righteousness. To the Corinthians Paul says, "Your boasting is not good. Don't you know that a little yeast works through the whole batch?"[71] Paul also warns the Galatians, "A little yeast works through the whole batch of dough."[72] Paul alludes to Jesus' warning about the affects of hiding sin in Matthew 13:33. This parable is often misunderstood but the

---
[70] Luke 12:1 (NIV)
[71] 1 Corinthians 5:6 (NIV)
[72] Galatians 5:9 (NIV)

meaning is not obscure: the result of the woman hiding leaven in the bushel of flour was that the whole amount became contaminated. Some translations say she *mixed* the leaven; but the meaning is *hid*.

The reason a woman might hide yeast is simply this: prior to the Passover, yeast had to be either used up or destroyed. Following Passover was the Feast of Unleavened Bread during which Israel could not eat leavened bread for a week. After the feast, it might take several days to reestablish the yeast starter.

In ancient bread making, there were no packets of yeast; rather a baker would hold back a portion of the dough to use as leaven on subsequent days. If you leave dough out, it will eventually collect yeast. San Francisco's sour dough bread tastes the way it does because of the yeast varieties common to the Bay Area.

With the Passover approaching, it would be tempting for someone to try to preserve her existing yeast until the end of the feast. What harm would there be? Nevertheless, Jesus is saying that in the kingdom economy, harboring sin leads to increasing corruption and eventual exposure just like hiding yeast in the flour.

The Corinthian church that Paul reprimanded was proud of its tolerance for a wicked member. Their prideful attitude said, *we are so patient, loving, and non-judgmental.* Paul tells them to expel him! Just as Jesus warned that hidden sin would permeate and pollute the Kingdom, Paul insists that we cannot manage around sin within the assembly. It is arrogant to allow room for it. It corrupts everyone who makes a place for it.

Remember that in his sin, Lucifer said, "I will ascend to heaven; I will raise my throne above the stars of God." Ezekiel says that Satan became proud because of his beauty. In the Garden of Eden the serpent tells Eve, "Your eyes will be opened, and you will be like God." Sin is arrogant; it is deceptive; it elevates the sinner above his Creator; it defies the Creator. Sin is leavening. Sin puffs up and it corrupts entirely, just as yeast permeates the whole loaf of bread and swells it to a size larger than it originally was. In contrast, Paul compares unleavened bread to sincerity and truth.

The unleavened bread of the Passover feast and of Eucharist is a symbol of Christ's body representing the absence of pride and the absence of sin. Jesus was perfect in his humility. He was entitled to glory, but he humbled

## The Sacrifice of Christ

himself instead. If Israel could not have yeast within its borders during Passover, the pre-cursor to the Lord's Supper, and if yeast symbolizes dishonesty, deceit, and pride, how much is it to expect that churches serve unleavened bread for the Lord's Supper? Paul tells the Corinthians,

> Clean out the old leaven so that you may be a new lump, just as you are in fact unleavened. Christ our Passover also has been sacrificed. Therefore let us celebrate the feast, not with old leaven, nor with the leaven of malice and wickedness, but with the unleavened bread of sincerity and truth.[73]

While Paul is speaking figuratively to the Corinthians, he is using elements from the traditions and practices that he taught them. He equates the unleavened bread of the feast with the purity of the church body and by inference the purity of Christ's body. Paul is speaking figuratively about an activity that the Corinthians practiced weekly. He communicates this way because the symbolism of their worship conveys meaning. Paul tells them that eating the Lord's Supper with members who are defiantly sinning is like celebrating the meal with leavened bread. He knows that they would not celebrate the Lord's Supper with leavened bread. Likewise, he tells them that their assembly must remain pure. Paul tells them to clean out the old leaven and celebrate the feast with sincerity and truth.

If the symbol of the Lord's body is unleavened bread, then it becomes very interesting when we realize that the symbol for the Lord's blood is wine. Wine is fermented grape juice. The organism, yeast, which is forbidden in the bread, is required to make the wine! The same yeast, which causes bread to rise, also causes wine to ferment. The Passover, which is the prototype of the Lord's Supper, forbids yeast bread. Nevertheless, the wine is a yeast product!

When we find such irony in Scripture, we should not run from it. We should investigate it. God was not oblivious to the irony when he instituted the feast. Nor would people in the first century be oblivious to the association of yeast and wine making. The Romans used the froth from the wine as a yeast starter for their bread.[xi] God designed this irony to instruct us, and so we will digress for a moment to consider the wine and the bread of the Lord's Supper more closely.

---

[73] 1 Corinthians 5:7, 8 (NASB)

# Chapter 3

When I attended Christian school years ago, a Bible teacher insisted that the wine at the Last Supper was non-alcoholic; he taught that it was just grape juice. Nothing in his mind could grasp that alcohol was not evil in and of itself. Of course, the New Testament teaches that food and drink are not evil. While gluttony and drunkenness are certainly sin, food and drink are not the cause; rather, substance abuse flows from our sin nature.

In Israel, the grape harvest and wine making occurred from July until September. The wine used at Passover would have been around for six months or more. It was fermented. Even if a variety of grape ripened in the early spring, the time it would take for grape juice to start fermenting is hours or even minutes. Solomon warned against drinking wine that is fermenting, "Do not gaze at wine when it is red, when it sparkles in the cup, when it goes down smoothly. In the end it bites like a snake and poisons like a viper."[74] Solomon was specifically talking about wine in which the yeast is still active creating bubbles as it ferments. His warning about alcohol abuse does not mean that alcohol is evil; in fact, Psalm 104 praises God, saying,

>He causes the grass to grow for cattle,
>And vegetation for the labor of man,
>So that he may bring forth food from the earth,
>**And wine which makes man's heart glad**,
>So that he may make his face glisten with oil,
>And food which sustains man's heart."[75]

As much as the Bible warns against drunkenness, it does not condemn drinking. In fact, Psalm 104 makes it clear that mild inebriating effects of wine are beneficial since it "makes man's heart glad." Psalm 104 equates wine with food. God recommended consumption of wine and other alcoholic beverages in the annual celebration of the tithe. God asked that people set aside ten percent of their increase to use as a festival of rejoicing. God told those who could not carry all their tithe, sell it and then buy food, alcoholic drink, or whatever they wanted when they arrived at the place where the ark of God was located. Read more about the tithe in Deuteronomy 14. The passage might surprise you.

---

[74] Proverbs 23:31, 32 (NIV)
[75] Psalm 104:14, 15 (NASB)

## The Sacrifice of Christ

Scripture does not condemn drinking wine any more than it condemns eating food. Jesus says of himself, "The Son of Man has come eating and drinking."[76] The drinking Jesus is referring to is wine. In fact, he turned the water into wine at the marriage feast at Cana. The religious Jews accused him of being a drunkard because they knew he consumed wine. Nevertheless, drinking and drunkenness are not the same.

Abusing any good thing is sin. Drunkenness and gluttony are both sins, but neither drinking nor eating is. Christians should not elevate petty prejudices in the face of Scripture. Doing so might make us hypocrites like the Pharisees whom Jesus scolded for elevating their traditions above the laws of God (Mark 7:8).

Wine is a gift from God and a powerful spiritual symbol. In the Old Testament sacrificial system, the priest poured out wine as a drink offering with the daily sacrifices. It may puzzle our self-righteous Evangelical-American sensibilities, but wine and alcohol consumption in general was an integral part of both the sacrifices and the feasts of the Jews as ordained by God and commanded by Moses. Just as Peter was told, "What God has cleansed, no longer consider unholy," Christians should temper their attitudes toward alcohol to be consistent with the whole record of Scripture and realize that it was an important part of Judaism and Christianity.

We should realize that commands to avoid abuse do not demand abstinence. In the Old Testament, abstinence from alcohol was the exception, not the rule. Likewise, in Christianity wine is at the center of the single recurring ordained celebration of the church, the Lord's Supper.

The wine at the Last Supper was the fully fermented finished product. If it had not finished fermenting, then it would have been in the process of fermenting and would have contradicted Solomon's warning. Modern wineries wash the yeast off the grapes in order to add varieties of yeast that produce desired qualities in the wine. In ancient times, the processes were not so sophisticated. Vintners crushed their grapes in a wine press hewn out of rock. They put the juice in clay jars until fermentation was complete.

Yeast in the New Testament always represents evil. Yeast works by breaking down the carbohydrates in the dough or in the juice. Simply put, it causes decay. No wonder Scripture uses yeast as a symbol of sin! Now

---
[76] Luke 7:34 (NASB)

certainly, yeast has beneficial effects, but the Bible draws attention to its ability to puff up while it destroys. The leaven of the Pharisees of which Jesus spoke reveals that they were puffed up, or arrogant, even as they were decaying spiritually.

The required element of the Lord's Supper consists of bread made without yeast, symbolizing the purity of Jesus Christ, and fermented wine, symbolizing the blood of Jesus. How can this be? If the unleavened bread represents perfection, why did God choose wine as a symbol for Christ's blood?

As soon as it is pressed, yeast infects the wine. How could this represent the precious blood of Jesus? For that matter, why do we commemorate Jesus' death with two symbols? The bread alone could represent his death and sacrifice. Why was it important to include wine as part of the picture?

Fortunately, God's symbols do not lie, nor are they redundant. Just as the Passover and the Day of Atonement reveal different perspectives of Christ's sacrifice, the bread and the wine also reveal different dimensions of Christ's sacrifice. The bread represents his sinless perfection. The wine represents his being made sin for us. The bread is without yeast to demonstrate his purity. Nevertheless, the wine made with yeast, symbolizes his blood sacrifice for sin.

The juice of the grape is free of yeast until the grape skin is crushed. Then yeast, which is already clinging to the grape skin, permeates the wine and ferments it. Likewise, Jesus was in the world surrounded by sinners, tempted by the devil, but without sin. He touched sinners; sinners touched him, but he remained without sin until his sacrifice on Calvary.

Just as the grape ferments when it is pressed, Jesus' perfect body when crushed became permeated with sin; not his sin, rather it became saturated with the sins of the entire world. When Jesus was in the Garden of Gethsemane the night before the Crucifixion he anguished over the burden of this. It was for this that he prayed, "My Father, if it is possible, may this cup be taken from me."[77] It was not the anticipation of physical pain that anguished him, but rather the understanding that he would bear the sins of the world. The cup he drank was the knowledge of sin.

---

[77] Matthew 26:39 (NIV)

# The Sacrifice of Christ

The Old Testament as well as Revelation, speak of the winepress of God's wrath. At the end of this last age, Christ will return to tread the winepress. He will destroy sin and rebellion by making war on the world and destroying those who rise up against him. The picture of the winepress of God's wrath is similar to the shedding of Jesus' blood on the cross. Both reveal the justice and righteousness of God. Both use wine as a symbol for blood and the judgment of sin. Nevertheless, Jesus' blood was a substitutionary sacrifice. Jesus' blood carried our sin. It bore our judgment. We have no fear of the winepress of God's wrath, because through the blood of Jesus Christ we have received mercy.

At the end of the sacrifice of Jesus Christ, the sins of the world are judged. The work of the devil, the deceit that held man in the fear of death, is destroyed. This was not a battle between good and evil. This was righteousness and judgment reconciling sinful man to his Creator God. Immediately before Jesus gives up his life he says, "It is finished. Father into your hands I commit my spirit!"[78] This was the one perfect God-Man acting in total obedience to his Father in heaven. In this, he paid the price for our salvation and secured our eternal redemption.

As wine finishes fermenting, alcohol destroys the yeast that caused fermentation. Likewise, Jesus' blood overcame the sin that he carried on the cross. Consequently, within the elements of the Lord's Supper we have a dimensional picture of the sacrifice of Christ. Unleavened bread symbolizes his purity and his worthiness as a sacrifice, while wine symbolizes his death and subsequent victory over sin!

The meaning of the Eucharist is not doggerel, such as, *Something white and something red . . .* or *Something wet and something dry . . .* The symbols represent so much more than color and texture. They also mean more than just flesh and blood. The unleavened and the leavened pictured together tell us that the one without sin was made to be sin for our sakes. Is that not the story that Scripture tells repeatedly in many different ways? Moses' bronze serpent, the scapegoat, and the Lord's Supper all symbolize Jesus' substitutionary sacrifice: not only his death, but also his becoming sin so to receive the judgment of sin in our place.

---

[78] John 19:30 and Luke 23:46 (NIV)

## Chapter 3

We should ask, how far must we depart from the original apostolic tradition before our sensibilities object? How calloused can we be? Should we not strive to conform to the original implementation of the one recurring feast that Christ commanded? Do the symbols encapsulate meaning or do they not? Do we celebrate the Lord's Supper or our own?

One might ask, *what about freedom in Christ*? We are free; we are free to celebrate or not to celebrate. Celebrating the Lord's Supper is not a requirement for salvation. Jesus said to do it as often as we do it for his remembrance. Nevertheless, because it is *his* remembrance and not our own, we are not free to alter the practice. Paul told the Corinthians that their celebration, which sowed division, was not even the Lord's Supper. Some were sick while others had died because they profaned the Lord's Supper. From 1 Corinthians 5 and 11 it is obvious that God expects a purity of practice. Modern churches, however, insist upon freedom of style.

We have stated that the Lord's Supper was first a Passover meal. From Christ's words, we can know that he intended continuity between the Passover and the Lord's Supper. Passover was the one feast that God commanded Israel to observe forever. Nevertheless, change for the Lord's Supper was appropriate because Jesus' sacrifice fulfilled the spiritual truth that the Passover foretold. Continuing to sacrifice animals would detract from what Jesus accomplished once for all.

The disciples on the evening of the Last Supper probably thought that *as often as you do it* meant annually at Passover; however, after Christ's resurrection local churches practiced the Lord's Supper weekly. Early Christians met together on the first day of the week for a full meal incorporating the bread and wine of the Eucharist. Acts 20 reveals that the reason they came together on the first day of the week was to "break bread" or to eat. It was not just something they did occasionally; it was the reason they came together. Ceremonial calendars no longer bind us, but rather we live in a daily relationship with the Lord and with each other. The Lord's Supper facilitates this.

1 Corinthians 14 tells the church how to conduct a meeting (since the third century most churches have altogether ignored its commands). It tells us what to do and how to do it. Also central to Paul's instruction to the Corinthians are details about the Lord's Supper. Most Evangelical churches

## The Sacrifice of Christ

having always ignored 1 Corinthians 14 treat the Lord's Supper as an afterthought: a once-a-month addendum to a regular service.

In 1 Corinthians 5 Paul emphasizes that the feast we celebrate is the Passover. Because Christ is our Passover lamb, we do not celebrate the feast with animal sacrifice, but we do celebrate it with unleavened bread. The unleavened bread is not only a symbol of Christ's body, but it is also a symbol of who we are. It is sadly ironic that Evangelical churches often celebrate just a facsimile of the Eucharist using yeast bread and unfermented grape juice. Are the symbols God has given us not suitable? Have we reduced the Eucharist to symbols of the symbols, pseudo-symbols?

Gabby sat between Lisa and me during a church service as they began to pass around the elements of communion (crackers and grape drink). She whispered to her mom, "Look, they're making a little snack." The snack idea has devolved from a misunderstanding of 1 Corinthians 11. Paul scolded the Corinthians for creating division in the celebration of the Lord's Supper. They came together to eat the Lord's Supper, and they did not celebrate with a snack but a full meal. However, some within the assembly were excluded from the meal and went away hungry; others over-indulged even to the point of drunkenness. It was inhospitable.

The Corinthian's practice did not picture the unity of the body that the one loaf and one cup symbolize. Paul told those that were *that* hungry to eat at home, but when the church assembled everyone should wait and eat together so there would not be division. Division was offensive because the purpose of gathering was to build unity in Christ. Paul's solution to the problem was not to turn the Lord's Supper into a *little snack*, but rather for people to eat it together with proper regard to the body of the Lord.

We might immediately think that the *body of the Lord* refers to his physical body, which he offered in sacrifice, and it does. Nevertheless, in the context of building unity, the *body of the Lord* also means his assembly. Ephesians 4 expounds on the concept of the church as the body of Christ. As we eat together, we are not to create division, but rather to acknowledge the Lord's body. At the Eucharist, we are not dwelling upon ourselves, but we are focusing on our relationship to Christ and to his body into which we are bonded together with other believers.

# Chapter 3

When we eat the little snack, we tend to be introspective. Our heads are bowed, and we ignore the social fellowship aspects of the Lord's Supper. Each one meditates upon his own thoughts and division is complete because we fragment the body into its component parts. There is no interaction among participants, and we share practically nothing except a crumb and a thimble. The elements of the Lord's Supper recall so much, and fellowship with believers builds unity, but what we practice today resembles neither the form nor substance of the weekly celebrations of the first century church and the New Testament.

Sin placed Adam and Eve under God's curse; God drove them from the Garden because they had damaged their relationship with God and entered into his judgment. They were now sinners and would now die because God made death to be the consequence of sin. Satan deceived Adam and Eve, and they were in bondage to sin; gripped by the fear of death under the judgment of God.

It was not from Satan's rebellion that God saved us, but from our own prideful sin. During the work of salvation, Jesus did not satisfy the demands of the devil as C. S. Lewis portrays in the Narnia allegory. Rather Jesus satisfied the demands of a holy and righteous God. The cross was not God's reaction to happenstance; it was his eternal plan. Jesus fulfilled that plan by offering his sinless body and his own blood as atonement for our sins. Through his work on the cross, Jesus reconciled us to the Father and bonded us together in his name. Christ's spirit, the Holy Spirit, now indwells us and consequently we are now Christ's body.

While God has restored our relationship to him, this change is to be manifest in our relationships to other believers. The epistles of John emphasize this. Our lives in Christ are manifest by our lives in his church, not by rote obedience to a top-down hierarchy, but by practicing equality and unity in love. He commanded us that we should eat together without division, and in our eating celebrate his mighty work of Salvation. Jesus offered his body as a sacrifice once for all, but as his redeemed, we are to celebrate his work continually through fellowship. If we really understood what Christ accomplished on Calvary, then we might celebrate the Lord's Supper more frequently and effectively.

## The Sacrifice of Christ

The elements of the Lord's Supper do not earn us merit or impart to us saving grace as some believe; nor are the elements literally the body and blood of the Lord Jesus. Nevertheless, the elements are powerful symbols and the Lord's Supper is more than a rote religious ritual. The Eucharist is real fellowship with Christ and with his church. It does recall Jesus' sacrifice, but it also looks forward to the Marriage Supper of the Lamb (Revelation 19:9), and, in the present, it celebrates the fact that believers are united in one body (1 Corinthians 10:17).

A proper celebration of the Lord's Supper centers our social relationships around Jesus; his sacrifice; his body, the church; and his promised return. In this regard, it is not only symbolic, but also practical. People nurture relationships over a meal. This is true in families, it is true in business, and it should be true in the church.

Knowing that he was calling a disparate people to represent him as his body in this world, he provides this instruction: *eat together*. How pragmatic! We are to eat together while remembering that we have him in common. We are pure because he was pure, and has made us pure. We are forgiven because he carried our sins. If we do this properly then there will be no division. If we do this we will be unified. Our relationship with God is redeemed; having a common bond with other believers, we realize the truth of Christ's body in our relationships.

Just as the blood of the lamb spared the Israelites from the angel of death on the first Passover, so Jesus Christ spares us from God's judgment by his sacrifice upon the cross. God delivered Israel from slavery in Egypt, just as he delivers us from the bondage of sin. Nevertheless, if the Israelites had not acted in faith and applied the blood to the lintel and doorposts, they would have perished like the Egyptians. The blood of the Passover lamb saved them from the Lord's angel of death. God spared the children of Israel from all the previous plagues that fell on Egypt. Nevertheless, at the Passover Israel was as vulnerable to the angel of death as Egypt was. The blood on the door caused the angel of death to pass over a home. Before they were released from the bondage of Egypt, Israel was first spared from the wrath of God by the sacrificial blood of a lamb.

Likewise, believers have been spared from the judgment of God. Who then is morally responsible for the act of the Crucifixion? Jesus did not nail

## Chapter 3

himself to the cross. The Jews and the Romans were responsible for their roles, but Paul makes it clear who is ultimately responsible, we are!

> Is not the cup of thanksgiving for which we give thanks a participation in the blood of Christ? And is not the bread that we break a participation in the body of Christ? Consider the people of Israel: Do not those who eat the sacrifices participate in the altar?[79]

By celebrating Eucharist, we acknowledge our role in the crucifixion. Charles Wesley, brother of John Wesley—founder of the Methodist Church, writes in his hymn, *Amazing Love:*

> And can it be that I should gain
> An interest in the Savior's blood?
> Died He for me, who caused His pain—
> For me, who Him to death pursued?
> Amazing love! How can it be,
> That Thou, my God, shouldst die for me?[xii]

Wesley understood on a personal level that he was a participant in the sacrifice. Wesley's sin was active at the altar. Not only was he a participant, he says he pursued it. We were, as was every man, present at the cross of the crucifixion. We pursued the Holy One to death at Calvary, and we should marvel as Wesley does at the outcome. The old spiritual, *Were You There*, is powerful because truly we were all there:

> Were you there when they crucified my Lord?
> Were you there when they crucified my Lord?
> Oh! Sometimes it causes me to tremble, tremble, tremble.
> Were you there when they crucified my Lord?[xiii]

Knowing our responsibility for the death of Christ and accepting his sacrifice for the atonement of our sins, we should seek now to live according to his will. In this, we follow his example and live for the sake of his body and not for ourselves.

---

[79] 1Corinthians 10:16, 18 (NIV)

## CHAPTER 4—THE WRATH OF MAN

*Fordid it. Jus', fordid it!*—Daniel age 2

The redemption story is a story of dimensions and contrasts. A Holy God redeems sinful man. The loving Creator rescues his rebellious, fallen creation. The offended forgives the offenders. The immortal God assumes a mortal existence. The sinless Christ becomes the sacrifice for sin. In the account of the Crucifixion, in particular, there are contrasts, that when examined, increase our understanding of the extent of God's love for man and the true character of man's rebellion against God.

The New Testament affirms Jesus' pre-incarnate participation in the Creation. Paul writes, "For us there is but one God, the Father, from whom are all things and we exist for Him; **and one Lord, Jesus Christ, by whom are all things**, and we exist through Him."[80] This tells us that what the Father ordained in Creation, the Son created, and the purposes that the Father has ordained for us are realized through the Son. John writes, "All things came into being through Him, and apart from Him nothing came into being."[81] Hebrews 1:2 tells us that God, "in these last days has spoken to us in His Son, whom he appointed heir of all things, through whom also He made the world."[82] The word that is translated *world* in Hebrews 1:2 is translated "eternity" and "beginning of time" elsewhere. The NIV translates

---
[80] 1 Corinthians 8:6 (NASB)
[81] John 1:3 (NASB)
[82] Hebrews 1:2 (NASB)

## Chapter 4

it, "through whom he made the universe." In truth, Christ created everything that ever was, is, or ever will be.

In the Creation account, God spoke the universe into existence. He even created animals by his command, "Let the water teem with living creatures" and "Let the land produce living creatures;" Nevertheless, in all creation one creature is special. Rather than speaking man into existence Genesis tells us, "The LORD God formed the man from the dust of the ground, and breathed into his nostrils the breath of life." Not only did God personally fashion the man, he made man in his own likeness. God also gave man a special mate, a woman, a female helper-companion whom he created from man's side.

Man, however, rebelled against the Creator. The world, which God the Father created through the Son, became hostile toward God and toward his righteousness. Into this hostile world, the Christ took upon himself the nature and identity of a man coexistent with his divinity. At the incarnation, he becomes a man; he does not just appear man-like as he had in Old Testament appearances. Jesus was a real man, not a spiritual apparition. Even now as Jesus Christ sits at the Father's right hand in Glory, he retains his human identity. The incarnation is an eternal change, which shows God's eternal commitment to the salvation of man.

In his original sin, man aspired to become god; nevertheless, in redemption God humbled himself, became a man, and destroyed all sin in his human body by his death. Jesus, the Son of God, is now also forever the Son of Man. Moreover, Paul tells the Philippians that Jesus, "Being found in appearance as a man, He humbled Himself by becoming obedient to the point of death, even death on a cross."[83] To paraphrase, because he was a man, Jesus submitted to die. Why does Paul say Jesus died? *Jesus died because he was a man and God had appointed man to die.* Man was condemned to die because of sin; nevertheless, Jesus had no sin. Because he had no sin, he could die for the sins of the world. His obedience opens up the possibility of reconciliation to God and righteousness by faith. At the Crucifixion, the love and mercy of God contrasts with the hostility and brutality of man.

---

[83] Philippians 2:8 (NASB)

# The Wrath of Man

## Consequences of the Curse

When man sinned against God in the Garden, God cursed man's relationships affecting the divine order of life. Sin distorts our relationships. God made man in God's own image but of the substance of earth. Man was God-like, but made from the earth. God designed man to rule the earth. The earth was his domain, but now with sin, and death that comes by sin, the man returns to the dust of the earth. The object that man was supposed to dominate instead reclaims the man's body to itself. This is no accidental irony. It is a reversal of the divine order caused by the curse of sin.

At the curse, God gave the woman pain in childbirth, and although her desire would be to fulfill the special God-designed relationship with her husband, her husband will now respond by ruling over her. Too many men read Genesis 3:16 and do not see it as a component of the curse. Some men prefer to see it as a mandate to dominate and control their wives. Some men use it as an excuse to divorce their wives who do not mechanically obey. Nevertheless, the literary parallels in the passage demonstrate that the husband's ruling over his wife can be nothing other than a curse upon the woman. While there is a natural divine order, it existed before the fall and was not punitive. Domination, or ruling over the woman, is hurtful and is a continuing consequence of sin. God designed man to dominate the earth, but instead he dominates his helper, the woman, his wife.

Perversely, some men allow their wives to dominate them, or some wives assert themselves above their husbands as if attempting to alleviate the curse. In battling the curse in this way, they also set themselves against the divine order. These attitudes of domination and rebellion create a circle of pain in which many married couples trap themselves.

Men also dominate rather than nurture their children. These dysfunctional relationships are symptomatic of the curse. Likewise, the Crucifixion reveals how severely sin has also distorted man's relationship with his Creator.

Jesus taught and ministered for three years often confronting the Jewish leaders about their hypocrisy and teaching people the truth about God. This angered the Jews and at times, they had tried to kill him. Jesus had escaped their wrath by walking away. This had surely been miraculous, but it was probably puzzling to the Jews. As Passover neared, the Jewish leaders were

# Chapter 4

again determined to kill Jesus to prevent him from carrying away the nation from their authority. At this time, Judas, a disciple, had also decided to betray him.

**The Days before the Cross**

Betrayal was the first treachery Jesus endured. The one who should be defending Jesus instead betrays him. Judas had seen the miracles that Jesus had performed. He had witnessed the power of God. Nevertheless, Judas, who was nothing without Jesus, presumes to elevate himself above his master just as Adam presumed to set his will above the will of God. A comparison of the Gospel accounts reveals the festering greed of Judas.

Twice while Jesus was in Bethany during the week before Passover, women anoint Jesus with very expensive perfume. At the first anointing Mary, the sister of Lazarus, anointed Jesus' feet with perfume and wiped them with her hair. This was similar to an anointing that occurred earlier in Jesus' ministry when he was in Galilee in the city of Nain. After Jesus raised a young man from the dead in the presence of the whole town, a sinful woman washed Jesus' feet with her tears and anointed them with perfume. Jesus told Simon the Pharisee at the time that her motivation was love, much love.

Mary, having also witnessed a resurrection by receiving her brother Lazarus back from the dead, now also expresses her love for Jesus by anointing his feet with expensive perfume. John mentions this anointing in the account of the resurrection of Lazarus thereby associating the resurrection of Lazarus and Mary's anointing of Jesus' feet. Can you imagine Mary thinking, *how can I say thank you, Lord?* Then recalling that after Jesus raised the child from the dead, the sinful woman anointed Jesus' feet, Mary decides to do the same. She takes perfume, which she had been saving, and she anoints Jesus' feet expressing her love and gratitude to him.

Mary anointed Jesus six days before the Passover according to John's Gospel. Jesus apparently arrived at Bethany on Friday afternoon and shared the Sabbath meal with Lazarus and his sisters. Mary anointed Jesus' feet after this meal. Judas was indignant because the perfume Mary used was worth a year's wages. He says, "Why was this perfume not sold for three hundred denarii and given to the poor?"[84] A denarii was a days wage. John

---

[84] John 12:5 (NASB)

## The Wrath of Man

makes it clear that Judas' motive was greed and theft. Judas had already purposed in his heart to betray Jesus, and since Judas controlled the moneybag, he stood to gain by Jesus' demise.

Jesus explains that Mary had kept this perfume to anoint him for burial. It is unclear whether Mary understood the symbolism of her act; nevertheless, it is clear from Jesus' words that the Holy Spirit motivated her actions.

Similarly, two days before the Passover, on a Tuesday evening, Jesus was still in Bethany but at Simon the Leper's house, and an unnamed woman came into the house and anointed Jesus' head with perfume. At Mary's anointing, she applied perfume to Jesus' feet. On this occasion, a woman pours the perfume over Jesus' head.

Some scholars assume that these are two accounts of the same event. Nevertheless, the first anointing occurred six days before Passover, the second occurred two days before Passover. Lazarus and his sisters hosted the meal at which the first anointing occurred. Simon the Leper hosted the meal at which the second anointing occurred. Mary anointed Jesus' feet, while the unnamed woman anointed his head. Judas grumbled at the first event, while *many* disciples grumbled at the second. The recorded facts diverge. There are similarities between the events: they occurred in Bethany, the perfume was expensive, and Jesus said the anointments were preparation for his burial. These similarities do not indicate that they were the same event. On the other hand, the timing, the location, and the difference between the anointments indicate that they are indeed two separate events.

The first anointing occurs before the Triumphal Entry. The second anointing occurs after the Triumphal Entry. Both Matthew and Mark tell us that immediately following this second anointing Judas went out and met with the chief priests and agreed to betray Jesus for 30 silver coins.

Prior to Judas' volunteering, the Jewish leaders had decided not to arrest Jesus during the feast for fear of the crowds, but Judas agreed to betray his master in such a way that the crowds would not see. This encouraged the Jews to accelerate their murderous scheme. Judas having lost the opportunity for financial gain twice in the same week now determines that he will exact a profit while there is still opportunity. He betrays his friend, his teacher, for a sum of money. His greed and anger at the

# Chapter 4

extravagance of Jesus' anointing compelled him. Although he had already decided to betray Jesus at some point, Jesus' anointing seems to have been the precipitating event that motivated Judas to action, an action that sent Jesus to the cross.

In the Old Testament, God prescribed a special perfumed ceremonial oil of anointing to consecrate the tabernacle, the priests, and later the kings of Israel. In the Bible an anointing confers upon the anointed a blessing and purpose. Moses anointed Aaron to be high priest of Israel. Samuel anointed David to be king of Israel. The Holy Spirit had already anointed Jesus: the title Christ means, "Anointed One."

Two days before his crucifixion, a woman anoints Jesus' head with perfumed oil. A priest or a prophet does not anoint him. The anointing comes from an unnamed woman. This woman was not the sinful woman who had washed his feet with her tears in Nain, nor was it Mary, sister of Lazarus who knew Jesus well, and anointed his feet with perfume and wiped them with her hair.

The woman who anointed Jesus' head is anonymous. Scripture records nothing else about her, but her story travels everywhere with the preaching of the Gospel. She is in a sense every righteous woman. Her actions echo back to Genesis and the promised seed of the woman who would crush the head of the serpent. Jesus was the promised seed of the woman. Therefore, the woman anoints Jesus' head as preparation for his burial. It is as if the woman is endorsing Jesus, saying, *He is the one of whom God spoke in the Garden.* Just as Moses' anointing of Aaron and Samuel's anointing of David conveyed purpose, so this anointing announces that Jesus has come into the world to die. Mary anointed his feet prior to the Triumphal Entry, steps that would lead to his death, and this anonymous woman anoints his head prior to his crowning with thorns.

The next evening after the Last Supper Jesus takes his disciples to the Garden of Gethsemane. He prays in this Garden with great anguish knowing what waits before him and says, "Father, if you are willing, take this cup from me; yet not my will, but yours be done."[85] Adam and Eve had betrayed God in the Garden of Eden by selling their innocence for the empty promise that they, too, would become like God. Jesus' choice in the Garden of Gethsemane

---

[85] Luke 22:42 (NIV)

# The Wrath of Man

put his Father's will above his own and he submits to the Father's will in perfect obedience. Paul says, "For as through the one man's disobedience the many were made sinners, even so through the obedience of the One the many will be made righteous."[86] The Garden of Gethsemane wherein Jesus chooses obedience recalls the context of Adam's choice of disobedience.

Judas brought the temple guards to the Garden of Gethsemane and there he kissed Jesus as if to mock their relationship. Jesus asked him, "Judas, are you betraying the Son of Man with a kiss?"[87] The disciples at first were ready to fight. One of them attacks a servant of the high priest and cuts off his ear. Jesus says, "Stop, no more of this," and heals the man who has come to arrest him. He then asks the Jews why they were arresting him at night since all week he had been teaching openly in the temple, which was within their jurisdiction. Their reasons reached into the depths of darkness beyond their own understanding. On the surface, they arrested Jesus at night because they were afraid of the crowds, but in truth, the treachery that would betray and arrest an innocent man when he was defenseless flowed from a heart of darkness: the darkness of man.

After Jesus' arrest, all his disciples deserted him including the remaining eleven. Mark, who was not one of the twelve but still a disciple, tells us that one young man, perhaps it was Mark himself, attempted to follow Jesus, but when he too was seized he escaped by leaving his clothes behind, fleeing naked into the night. Peter follows at a distance, but before dawn, he has denied knowing Jesus three times. Through his trial Jesus stands alone deserted even by those who should have loved him the most.

**The Trial**

At the time of Jesus' crucifixion, there were two high priests in Judah, Annas and his son-in-law, Caiaphas. Annas ran the temple as an organized crime racket. Remember that on the day of the Triumphal Entry as well as on the day after, Jesus had disrupted the business in the temple using physical force to drive away merchants and moneychangers. He quoted Jeremiah saying, "My house will be called a house of prayer, but you are making it a den of robbers."[88] As a crime boss, Annas would have had unscrupulous

---
[86] Romans 5:19 (NASB)
[87] Luke 22:48 (NASB)
[88] Matthew 21:13 (NIV)

## Chapter 4

dealings with the Romans also. In fact, the Romans held sway over the high priest to insure his allegiance to the Roman government. Consequently, Annas was both a puppeteer and a puppet.

Although the high priest was supposed to serve for his entire life, the Romans had deposed Annas: perhaps he had over-reached and cheated the wrong Roman. Perhaps his crimes had made him unpopular with the people forcing the Romans to intervene and remove him from the office of high priest while leaving him in charge of the criminal enterprise from which they also benefited.

Annas' sons also served as high priest at one time or another. We do not know what specific political or economic expedience put Caiaphas in the role of high priest; however, both Annas and Caiaphas were priests according to the line of Aaron. The high priesthood of Aaron of the tribe of Levi had a beginning at Sinai and each high priest could serve only as long as he was alive, obviously. Their service had a beginning and an end.

The Sadducees, of which were Annas and Caiaphas, did not believe in the resurrection of the dead or in the eternal punishment of sin. Being priests in Israel was to them their own good fortune since they profited from the ritual temple worship. In a sense, they did not worship God, but rather they worshipped themselves because they enriched themselves at the expense of the devout.

In the middle of the night Jesus stood before the two chief priests. Hebrews tells us that Jesus was a high priest according to the order of Melchizedek. Jesus' priesthood had no beginning and no end unlike the Levitical priesthood inherited by Annas and Caiaphas. The writer of Hebrews also tells us that the priesthood of Melchizedek was the greater priesthood as well. Abraham had tithed his spoils of battle to Melchizedek, and Hebrews says that Levi also tithed to Melchizedek because he was still in Abraham's loins at this time. Consequently, all priests from the line of Aaron were in an inferior position to the high priest, Jesus Christ.

Therefore, Jesus, the Great High Priest, stands accused before two lesser chief priests. Jesus is questioned in front of Annas. When his answers are not satisfactory, his captors strike Jesus in the face while his hands are bound. Annas then sends Jesus to Caiaphas, who was acting high priest that year. According to the Law, the high priesthood should have gone to Annas' oldest

## The Wrath of Man

son upon his death. Caiaphas is Annas' son-in-law and Annas is still alive. Therefore, Jesus, the high priest according to Melchizedek stands trial before an imposter or usurper.

Before Caiaphas and the rest of the Jewish council, many people falsely accuse Jesus. Nevertheless, their testimony does not corroborate any accusation against Jesus. Apparently missing from the accusations is an account of Jesus clearing the temple of the merchants and moneychangers. Jesus was justified in his clearing the temple because the temple was his house. Nevertheless, had witnesses testified of that, they would have implicated the whole temple system in court. Perhaps some more devout Pharisees would have seized that opportunity to impugn the record of Annas and the Sadducees.

Amidst the false accusations, Jesus stood before Caiaphas silently. While Jesus had given testimony to Annas, he apparently shows Caiaphas no similar respect. Jesus, who is the truth, and the life, stands on trial for his life in a dishonest court where liars accuse him and imposters judge him, and he is silent. Finally, Caiaphas asks him directly, "Are you the Christ, the Son of the Blessed One?" Jesus who has not responded to false accusations, at this replies, "I am. And you will see the Son of Man sitting at the right hand of the Mighty One and coming on the clouds of heaven."[89] Jesus was not interested in defending against lies; that would only distract from the truth he wanted to speak. He was intent upon declaring the truth and he waited for the appropriate time.

Upon hearing this, Caiaphas tore his robes, ended the trial, and pronounced Jesus guilty of blasphemy. Some of the men, either members of the council or perhaps the temple guards, blindfolded Jesus. They spit on him and they struck him on the face saying, "Prophesy! Who hit you?" Nevertheless, Jesus is silent.

Before the morning of Passover dawns, the Jewish mob including the chief priests and the council, called the Sanhedrin, brings Jesus before Pilate, the Roman governor of Judea. Because Pilate is a Gentile, and because it is a festival week, the Jews would not enter his palace. They believed that they would not be ceremonially clean for Passover if they had.

---

[89] Mark 14:61, 62 (NIV)

# Chapter 4

Pilate comes out on his portico in the middle of the night to hear their accusations, and then takes Jesus inside the palace and questions him. Jesus answers Pilate's questions, but Pilate finds no fault in Jesus. He learned that Jesus was from Galilee and so he sends him to Herod the tetrarch, the governor of Galilee, who is visiting Jerusalem. Herod's father, Herod the Great, built the palace in Jerusalem where the Roman governors lived. Herod the Great was also the king who tried to kill Jesus after the Magi came looking for the Christ child.

The geography of the trial and crucifixion is compressed. Any point within the temple complex is within a couple tenths of a mile of any other place. Travel from one place to another would have only taken a few minutes. A bridge called the royal porch spanned the distance between the temple and the palace.

Herod, who had ordered the execution of John the Baptist, had also been curious about Jesus. Herod had been both humored and annoyed by John's prophesies. He wanted to see Jesus perform miracles, but Jesus is silent before Herod. Herod and his soldiers mocked Jesus. They dressed him in royal robes before sending him back to Pilate.

When Jesus came back to Pilate, Pilate tried to release him, but the anger of the Jews was unsettling to Pilate. Pilate's wife sent him a message telling him that Jesus was innocent and that she had nightmares on Jesus' account. Pilate, though, left it up to the Jews. He tells the Jews he will release a brutal thief and murderer named Barabbas, or Jesus, their choice. The Jews, however, would not relent and insisted that Pilate crucify Jesus. Consequently, Pilate sentences Jesus to death and releases Barabbas. This detail also demonstrates the substitutionary death of Jesus Christ. Barabbas, the criminal, is freed while Jesus, the innocent, is condemned.

This all occurred in darkness before sunrise as secretly and as urgently as possible. Since the previous evening, Jesus had been betrayed, disowned, and deserted by friends. As a high priest after Melchizedek, Jesus had stood silently through false accusations before two Jewish chief priests. Jesus stood also before two Roman governors; Herod was curious about miracles, but had no interest in justice. Pilate would have preferred justice, but his self-interest dictated that Jesus be crucified even though Pilate's wife had warned him about her disturbing dreams. Throughout the events leading up to the

## The Wrath of Man

Crucifixion, everyone whom Jesus encounters looks out for his own best interests. Judas betrays him. Peter disowns him. John and the other disciples desert him. The priests reject him as Messiah to preserve their status and enterprises. Pilate ignores justice to preserve order and authority. Herod was amused and then bored by Jesus. He did not carefully weigh his innocence. Nevertheless, Jesus had come to earth for this purpose to die even for the sins of those who abused him.

## The Crucifixion

Pilate sentenced Jesus to death by crucifixion, and washed his hands as a symbol of his personal reluctance to kill an innocent man, but more so as a refusal to take responsibility. Regardless of how distraught he might have seemed, Pilate was the type of man who is willing to make the hard choice to serve his own best interests. The Jewish leaders probably held sway over Pilate and so he felt he must capitulate. With Herod visiting Jerusalem, Pilate probably felt pressure to appease the Jewish leaders. Pilate had governorship of Judea because Herod's brother had been incompetent. Pilate would not have wanted Herod to make a case against him. In fact, Luke tells us that on that day Pilate and Herod became friends.

The Romans beat Jesus severely. Isaiah prophesied of the suffering Christ saying, "His appearance was marred more than any man and His form more than the sons of men."[90]

Why is this detail important? *The Son of God, in the Creation formed man after his image. At the crucifixion, sinful men beat the Son of God so severely that he no longer resembles a man.* This irony is not coincidental; rather, it reveals the depth of the Savior's love for man and the darkness of man's sinful nature. What God formed in love, sin deforms in hatred.

Other ironies of the Crucifixion demonstrate the contrasts between a righteous, loving God and sinful, hostile man. The psalmist, David, writes prophetically of the Crucifixion in the first person saying, "I am poured out like water, and all my bones are out of joint."[91] In the celebration of Sukkoth, or the Feast of Tabernacles, which foreshadowed Jesus coming in the flesh, the officiating priest pours out water into a basin by the altar. The water

---

[90] Isaiah 52:14 (NASB)
[91] Psalm 22:14 (NASB)

drained to the base of the altar along with wine from the drink offering which a priest poured out in its own basin. The pouring out of water was a prayer of salvation for the nation of Israel. The Psalmist prophetically compares this pouring out with the crucifixion of Jesus Christ. Jesus' face was beaten, his beard was torn out, and on the cross, his bones were pulled out of joint.

This disfigurement contrasts with the beauty and majesty that the Creator bestowed upon man by forming the man in the image of God. Nevertheless, Jesus endured this disfigurement, this torture, for the benefit of man, indeed for the salvation of man. It is the fulfillment of all the prayers throughout the ages for the salvation of Israel. However, it comes at a price that not even the prophets themselves understood. Jesus, the Son of God, is poured out like water. Their prayer for salvation through the ages culminates at the pouring out of the Son of God.

At the Crucifixion, Roman soldiers nailed Jesus' hands and feet to the cross. The cross commemorates Adam's choice to sin against God. The cross was to Jesus the Tree of Knowledge of Good and Evil that Adam had chosen in defiance of God. Whereas Adam had taken the fruit of the tree in disobedience, Jesus now endures the tree because of his obedience. Upon the cross Jesus, who knew no sin, becomes sin. The first tree was a living tree in a splendid garden, the second was a dead tree raised up in a place called Golgotha, or the place of the skull. Adam ate the fruit of the Tree of Knowledge of Good and Evil. The cross now becomes the cup of the knowledge of sin to a sinless Christ.

The hands of sinful men now nail the hands of the Creator to this tree. The hands of him who sculpted man from the earth stretched out across the beam while men abused them. At Calvary, the creature drives nails through the hands of his Creator. This pictures the bitterness of sin.

In the Psalms, the hand of God represents strength, refuge, salvation, justice, provision, blessing, and kindness toward man. The malignancy of man's sin responds to kindness by piercing the hands of Jesus Christ. Such a treacherous act displays for us the depth of Jesus' love. He would endure such injury and insult to reconcile sinful man to his Creator.

Men also nailed to the cross the feet of him who had walked with Adam and Eve in the Garden of Eden. In the Psalms, God's feet represent his absolute authority and his judgment. Now God's friendship is spurned, his authority is reviled, and his judgment judged by sinners with the cruelty upon his feet.

The Creator, who had furnished sinful man garments to cover his shame, men now stripped naked for all to see. The Psalmist also prophesied of this moment saying,

> Dogs have surrounded me;
> A band of evil men has encircled me,
> They have pierced my hands and feet.
> I can count all my bones;
> **People stare and gloat over me.**
> **They divide my garments among them**
> **And cast lots for my clothing.**[92]

The Roman death squad did exactly what the psalmist wrote; Mark records it most succinctly: "They crucified him. Dividing up his clothes, they cast lots to see what each would get."[93] The Creator had covered Adam and Eve's shame. Man now answers that mercy by exposing the body of the Savior. Jesus hangs naked; sinful men mock him. Those who have reason to be ashamed, cast shame upon him who has nothing of which to be ashamed.

Within these ironies of the Crucifixion is an attention to detail. The face, the hands, the feet, the disfigured and exposed body of our Lord all recall the Son's actions in Creation and in the Garden of Eden.

On Jesus' cross, Pilate had placed a sign written in Aramaic, Latin, and Greek that proclaimed, "JESUS OF NAZARETH, THE KING OF THE JEWS." Jesus was indeed in line to be the king of the Jews. Jesus' testimony had convinced Pilate that he was indeed the king of the Jews. Pilate asked the priests and the council, "Then what shall I do with Jesus who is called Christ?" John says that Pilate's final appeal on behalf of Jesus was this: "Shall I crucify your king?" The Jews cried out, "We have no king, but Caesar." Men led Jesus to the place of the skull as he wore the royal garments with which Herod had dressed him. For a crown, the Roman soldiers had fashioned a crown of thorns. Thorns are a symbol of the curse that man's sin brought upon the earth; and here in the hour of his coronation and execution, the symbol of the curse of sin crowns the Righteous One.

---

[92] Psalm 22:16-18 (NIV)
[93] Mark 15:24 (NIV)

# Chapter 4

When the high priest made the annual sacrifice for the sins of the nation of Israel at Yom Kippur, or the Day of Atonement, with his hands he symbolically laid the sins of the nation upon the head of the scapegoat. The priest then led goat the outside the camp or outside the city to die. At the crucifixion, men crown Jesus' head with the symbol of the sins of the whole world before leading him outside the city to crucify him.

Death upon a cross came gradually by exhaustion, dehydration, and ultimately suffocation. The exposure to elements, the cold or heat, would diminish the victim's strength. Hanging would make breathing difficult and the accompanying physical trauma would cause dehydration.

On the day of Jesus' Crucifixion, the Jews sought to shorten the duration of the executions so that the bodies would not be hanging during Passover. Their sensitivity to the formalities of their religion is ironic considering they had crucified the Lord of Glory. Pilate ordered the legs of the men crucified to be broken. This would cause suffocation to come more quickly as the victims struggled to breathe against the weight of their own bodies.

On the cross, Jesus would have struggled to breathe even though his legs were never broken. The pain of the nails in his feet and hands versus the suffocating effects of hanging made every breath excruciating. Thinking back to the creation we remember that the Creator breathed into man the breath of life. Now the creature slowly suffocates the Creator as if to extinguish the very breath of life from its source.

The psalmist declares, "By the word of the LORD the heavens were made, And by the breath of his nostrils all their hosts."[94] Now he who had made even the heavens and the heavenly hosts by his own word and his breath is now struggling to speak and breathe. The crucifixion continues to paint a contrasting picture of man's extreme malice and God's greater love.

Upon the cross, Jesus cried out, "I thirst!" He who had caused a mist to water the Garden of Eden, he who had sweetened the waters of Marah, he had made water flow from a rock at Meribah so that Israel would not die of thirst, is now dying and thirsty.

The blood loss from the trauma has left Jesus parched. The Psalmist describes this prophetically saying, "My strength is dried up like a potsherd,

---

[94] Psalm 33:6 (NASB)

## The Wrath of Man

and my tongue sticks to the roof of my mouth; you lay me in the dust of death."[95]

At Marah in the wilderness, the children of Israel had come to a place where the water was bitter and undrinkable. The Lord had shown Moses a tree, and upon Moses' throwing the tree into the water, the water became sweet. Now hanging upon a tree, Jesus through his thirst cries out, and in response, men give him bitter vinegar to drink. Man repays sweetened water with bitter vinegar.

At the Crucifixion, we see the kindness of God toward man reversed into cruelty toward the Son of God. The malice revealed against Jesus is especially engineered as an affront to the deity of Jesus Christ. The disfigurement of his face and body, his nakedness, the piercing of his hands and his feet, the crown of thorns on his head, his struggles to breathe, and the dire thirst he experienced all seem to target and insult his identity as Creator.

Was this pure malice aforethought by the Jews and Romans to punish the Creator? No, Paul says that God ordained it. He says,

We speak God's wisdom in a mystery, the hidden wisdom which
God predestined before the ages to our glory; the wisdom which
none of the rulers of this age has understood; for if they had
understood it they would not have crucified the Lord of glory.[96]

Jesus prayed from the cross, "Father, forgive them, for they do not know what they are doing."[97] So if man acted in ignorance why was his treatment of Jesus so perfectly treacherous? If God ordained Christ's suffering, why was it so incredibly cruel?

On the cross, Jesus took upon himself the sins of the world. Paul says, "He [God] made Him who knew no sin to be sin on our behalf, so that we might become the righteousness of God in Him."[98] The treachery that Jesus endured demonstrates to us the depth and consequences of our sin. Without the treachery, Christ's death would not have pictured the festering disease of sin.

That is not to say that God suffers each time we sin, but rather that our sin is violently offensive to him. Peter, Paul, and the writer of Hebrews make

---
[95] Psalm 22:15 (NIV)
[96] 1 Corinthians 2:7, 8 (NASB)
[97] Luke 23:34 (NASB)
[98] 2 Corinthians 5:21 (NASB)

## Chapter 4

it clear that Jesus suffered and died once for all. Hebrews warns against those who by their falling away would again crucify the Son of God. The cross is for us a picture of our own sin, but it would be errant to claim that Jesus Christ suffers again each time we sin. Christ suffered and died once for all time and his blood atoned for everyone's sin past, present, and future.

Nevertheless, when we sin, we do not sin unto ourselves. We do not sin only against other people. When we sin, we sin against God. The insult of sin existed long before the acts of the Crucifixion. The Crucifixion pictures for us the horror and depravity of our own sin. Our sin disfigured the one who created us in his image. Our sin pierced the hands of the Creator who formed us. Our sin sought to suffocate him who breathed into us the breath of life. Our sin shamed him who had covered our shame. Our sin parched him who said, "If anyone is thirsty let him come to me and drink."[99] Our sin crowned the Creator with the symbol of our curse. Our sin mocked him who comforted us. Our sin taunted him who heals us. Our sin crucified him who loved us. The cross of Jesus Christ should cause us to despise our own sin and our own sin nature. It should motivate us to die to sin and live for God.

If the Crucifixion shows us the extent of our own depravity, it also shows us the depth of God's love and mercy. Jesus, while suffering, asked the Father to forgive the Roman death squad and the jeering crowd. He could endure the crucifixion for the joy of reconciling fallen man to himself. The Crucifixion shows us that the Creator would endure the wrath of man so that man could escape the wrath of God. Psalm 76:10 prays to God, "Surely the wrath of man shall praise thee." Consequently, God ordained the accomplishment of his purpose, not in spite of man's disobedience, but through man's disobedience! Through the cross, which revealed the total malignancy of sin, God begins his greatest work, which is the redemption of man by the salvation of his soul.

Man crucifies Jesus, but Jesus does not die by the will of man. Jesus said of his death, "I lay down my life so that I may take it again. No one has taken it from Me, but I lay it down on My own initiative."[100] And so it was that when the time had come, Jesus called out, "'Father, into your hands I commit my spirit.' Having said this, he breathed his last."[101] Jesus endured the

---
[99] John 7:37 (NASB)
[100] John 10:17, 18 (NASB)
[101] Luke 23:46 (NASB)

## The Wrath of Man

suffering men inflicted upon him, but his death came about of his own volition in submission to the will of God. That is not to say that his wounds were not fatal, or that men bore no responsibility. Peter preaches of the Crucifixion saying, "We are witnesses of everything that he did in the country of the Jews and in Jerusalem. They killed him by hanging him on a tree."[102] But even though fatal wounds were inflicted by man, it is Jesus who has submitted to crucifixion and it is he who gives up his spirit to God the Father.

When the soldiers came to hasten Jesus' death by breaking his legs they found that he had already died. Jesus' legs were not broken thus fulfilling a prophecy found in Psalm 34 and fulfilling the type of the Passover lamb, which could have no bones cut or broken. To confirm his death a soldier pierced Jesus' side with a spear and out flowed water mixed with blood. This picture is a poignant reminder of the Feast of Sukkoth and the pouring out of water and wine with the morning sacrifice.

Sukkoth, or Feast of Tabernacles, foreshadowed Jesus' incarnation. John says that Jesus "*tabernacled* among us." The NIV translates the phrase "made his dwelling among us", but the word used is the word for tabernacle. A tabernacle, or sukkah, was a temporary dwelling in which the children of Israel lived for seven days during the feast, which occurs in late September or early October. A sukkah's roof was at least partially open to the sky. It typifies both Jesus' incarnation and our temporary sojourn upon this earth. Some believe that Jesus was born during the Feast of Sukkoth rather than on or around December 25. If this is the case, then December 25 (Hanukah according to the Gregorian calendar) corresponds to the angel's announcement to Mary rather than the actual birthday of Jesus. In truth, it is always an appropriate time to remember that Jesus came to earth to tabernacle among us.

In ancient Israel, a drink offering poured out near the altar accompanied each sacrifice offered by the priests of Israel, but at Sukkoth, there was also the pouring out of water. The sacrifices of Sukkoth, like all the sacrifices in the Old Testament typify Jesus' death in some way. At Calvary, blood and water spill on the ground at the base of the cross signifying that the prayers of Sukkoth throughout the ages are answered. Jesus' death was the fulfillment of all the sacrifices since they had begun.

---

[102] Acts 10:39 (NIV)

# Chapter 4

**The Eucharist in Reflection**

At the Lord's Supper, we remember the body and the blood of Jesus. The unleavened bread represents his holy, sinless body. The wine, fermented by yeast, represents Jesus' blood that he offered as a sacrifice for sin. Just as the wine destroys the yeast that ferments it, so Jesus' blood vanquishes the sin of man.

The Lord's Supper remembers Jesus' sacrifice at Calvary, and it looks forward to his triumphant return. In the interim, we contemplate the meaning of the sacrifice and our role therein. Paul asks,

> Is not the cup of thanksgiving for which we give thanks a participation in the blood of Christ? And is not the bread that we break a participation in the body of Christ? . . . Consider the children of Israel: Do not those who eat the sacrifices participate in the altar?[103]

The actors in the Crucifixion from the disciples to the rulers to the mobs all revealed their own attitude toward Jesus. However, not intentionally, they participated in the altar. There were those who hated him and those who loved themselves more. Examining the Crucifixion we, too, must take a position about Jesus, about who we believe he is and about what we believe our response must be. Jesus did not die for only the sins of the Jews and the Romans. He died for our sins, too. How do we respond? Herod thought there was entertainment value to seeing Jesus; perhaps Jesus would perform a miracle. When Jesus did not perform on cue Herod mocked him. The Jews had already decided that they wanted to kill Jesus. His testimony was more than just inconvenient to them; his life was a threat to their illicit livelihood. Pilate could see the injustice of crucifying an innocent man, but ultimately he chose to act according to his own interests. Jesus' disciples betrayed, disowned, and deserted him.

At Calvary, there was the dying thief who asked Jesus to remember him. Perhaps the thieves on either side of Jesus were companions of Barabbas whom Pilate had freed.

We, like the thieves, are dying. Though we are not under the sentence of death by a Roman court, we are all under the sentence of death by God against whom we have sinned. Interposed between our guilt and the

---

[103] 1 Corinthians 10:16, 18 (NIV)

righteous judgment of God is the cross of Jesus Christ. How we respond to Jesus' sacrificial death on the cross will determine whether he remembers us at the coming of his kingdom, or whether we suffer the wrath of God, which we no doubt deserve.

The dying thief expressed a fear of God. He admitted that he was sinful and that he deserved to die. The thief acknowledged that Jesus was a righteous man and he believed that the cross was not the outcome but the beginning of something more. He asked, "Jesus, remember me when You come into Your kingdom!" Upon hearing that request Jesus assured him, "I tell you the truth, today you will be with me in paradise."[104] *Paradise* might be translated, *the garden*. And so, the drama of the cross has brought us full circle: from the garden where man disobeyed, to the garden where Jesus obeyed, to the garden where man will find reconciliation and healing.

When we come to Jesus in faith, we also come to our own cross. Jesus said, "If anyone wishes to come after Me, he must deny himself, and take up his cross daily and follow Me."[105] Likewise, Paul says,

> If we have become united with Him in the likeness of His death, certainly we shall also be in the likeness of His resurrection, knowing this, that our old self was crucified with Him, in order that our body of sin might be done away with, so that we would no longer be slaves to sin; for he who has died is freed from sin.[106]
> I have been crucified with Christ; and it is no longer I who live, but Christ lives in me; and the life which I now live in the flesh I live by faith in the Son of God, who loved me and gave Himself up for me.[107]

In accepting our cross, we give up our lives to follow Jesus; nevertheless, the gains for us far outweigh the costs. We will die, our mortal bodies will come to ruin. Ecclesiastes tells us that everything we accomplish in this life is meaningless apart from pleasing God. At salvation, we agree to crucify the flesh and live by faith in Jesus Christ instead. The gift of salvation is free, but it has a price. The grace of God is not earned, but it is not cheap.

---

[104] Luke 23:42-43 (NIV)
[105] Luke 9:23 (NASB)
[106] Romans 6:5-7 (NASB)
[107] Galatians 2:20 (NASB)

# Chapter 4

Sometimes so-called Christians preach a cheap grace that is free and costs us nothing but gains us everything we desire. Such an attitude fails to understand what Christ did. Christ did for us what we could not do for ourselves; he reconciled us to God the Father. If we believe, we need to continue with that pattern. Just as we receive salvation by faith, for there is no other way, we are to live our lives by faith trusting God in every situation. This is hardly cheap grace because it commits us to a lifelong journey whereby we learn to walk in faith.

We cannot continue to live for ourselves; attempting to do so denies our Creator and elevates ourselves. Modern Christianity often teaches that the Christian life is a source of power wherein we can accomplish anything that we desire. This is not true. This philosophy elevates the will of the individual over the will of God. Some teach that our will is God's will because Jesus left the planet and put us in charge. Self-empowerment is the essence of the sin in the Garden of Eden when Adam and Eve chose to become like gods. The face, hands, feet, and body of Christ on the cross picture for us the underlying attitude of our sin. Our sin, our self-interest, is an affront to our Creator, but his gift is the blessing of eternal life to us. Therefore, as we continue in the faith that saved us, we will continue to see our insufficiency and look to Jesus in faith to be our sufficiency in every aspect of our lives.

Matthew 13 gives us the *Parables of the Kingdom*. Two of them, the parable of the *hidden treasure* and the parable of the *costly pearl* present a converse relationship between God's love for believers and the believer's love for his God. The man sells all that he has to buy a field containing a treasure. This story pictures Christ's sacrifice to redeem us, while the merchant who seeks many pearls until he finds the one of great value pictures our commitment to Christ. Whatever wisdom the world offers we willingly discard in order to gain the hidden wisdom of Christ.

Too often modern Christianity treats the sacrifice of Jesus Christ lightly. The path to salvation to some is just a magical incantation that neither fully confesses who Christ is, nor fully commits one's life to him. We should be careful to understand the true nature of our salvation. The blood of Jesus Christ redeems us from the wrath of God. It changes us because we too die with him on the cross. Paul says, "Your body is the temple of the Holy Spirit who is in you, whom you have from God, and you are not your own for you

## The Wrath of Man

have been bought with a price: therefore glorify God in your body."[108] Peter writes, "He himself bore our sins in his body on the tree, so that we might die to sins and live for righteousness, by his wounds you have been healed."[109] The healing of which Peter is speaking is not healing from every physical illness as some preach. The healing to which Peter refers is the healing that allows us to live for righteousness: the healing is our reconciliation to God. While God can and does heal the physical body, the healing of reconciliation is much richer than mere healing from illness or injury. A healed relationship with God is forever, while physical healing is temporary.

The physical suffering and death of Jesus Christ brings about a spiritual reality in our lives today; nevertheless, we still await a physical fulfillment of the promise of our own resurrection. In our new life, we learn to watch for what God is doing and pray for wisdom to see and do his will rather than to strive for what we want and beg him to capitulate to our demands.

Another error regarding the doctrine of Salvation imagines that we must merit the grace that we receive, as if our good deeds and devotion earn us the grace that saves us. This man-centered salvation is a continuation of the sin in the Garden whereby man sought to elevate his importance. By elevating man's role, we diminish both the power and mystery of the heart of God. He created us, he chose us, he redeemed us, and he sustains us. He does all this for his own purposes and for his own pleasure.

The bread and the wine that we consume at The Lord's Supper look back to the Crucifixion. They commemorate the body and blood of our Lord so that we can remember that we also participated in the altar. It was for our sins that he died. He endured our wrath. He caused man's wrath to glorify himself by offering through it the sacrifice of reconciliation.

Jesus told his disciples at the Last Supper, "I will not drink of this fruit of the vine from now on until I drink it anew with you in my Father's kingdom."[110] Paul writes, "Whenever you eat this bread and drink this cup, you proclaim the Lord's death until he comes."[111] Consequently, the Lord's Supper also looks forward to Jesus' coming and to our own resurrection. In eternity, we will still celebrate what started at Passover, but then we will

---

[108] 1 Corinthians 6:19, 20 (NASB)
[109] 1 Peter 2:24 (NIV)
[110] Matthew 26:29 (NIV)
[111] 1 Corinthians 11:26 (NIV)

## Chapter 4

celebrate around the Lord's Table all that he has done for us in creation, redemption, and reconciliation.

At that time, we will no longer have a sin nature, and we will no longer have conflicts between our old sin nature and our new life in the Spirit. Our earthly body resurrects into a heavenly body without the constraints and without the curse of sin. Our healing and reconciliation to God will be complete. In the resurrection, we will also understand fully what we can barely grasp now.

The resurrection is our hope. All earthly things pale in comparison to this, and it is this hope that keeps our faith focused on him who loved us enough to take all our sin upon himself so that we could become the righteousness of God through him.

In Matthew 16, after Peter made his famous confession to Jesus saying, "You are the Christ, the Son of the Living God." Jesus commended Peter's faith. He indicated that upon that confession he would establish his church, or his assembly. He said, "The gates of Hades will not overpower it."[112] This was his first direct mention of the church and the first direct promise *to* the church.

Unfortunately, Jesus' words are largely misunderstood. Some people suppose that the church is defensive and the kingdom of hell will not overcome it. Others presume that the gates of hell are defensive and the church mounts an assault upon the kingdom of hell. Both of these interpretations are preposterous fantasies. Scripture never mentions any *kingdom of hell*; consequently, the kingdom of hell is a theological fiction. So what did Jesus mean when he said, "The gates of Hades will not overpower it"?

Jesus was speaking to his disciples in the Greek language in a culture that was heavily influenced by Greece and Rome. Should we not attempt to understand his words in their context? Moreover, Jesus was telling them about his *εκκλεσια*, which means *assembly* and is usually translated *church*. Ekklesia was a Greek political structure used in local government where all men had equal voice. Jesus also knew that within a few years his assembly would consist mostly of Gentiles. *Hades* is the Greek word for the place of the

---

[112] Matthew 16:16, 18 (NASB)

## The Wrath of Man

dead or the underworld. Hades was not necessarily a place of suffering; it was the realm of the dead, or the grave.

According to the Greek understanding, the gates of Hades were guarded by Cerberus, a three-headed dog. Cerberus would not permit those in Hades to pass again through the gates into the realm of the living. Death was consequently a hopeless state. Jesus was using this literary or cultural allusion to illustrate his first promise to his church.

At his very first mention of his church, Jesus promises resurrection to all who confess to him, "You are the Christ, the Son of the Living God." Death cannot keep us. The grave will not hold us. The gates of Hades will not overcome us.

Jesus promises that we will rise again!

# CHAPTER 5—THE RESURRECTION

*"The water was cold, but I wanted to obey Jesus."* — Cara age 5
*"Let no one take your crayon."* — Cara age 4
*"I'm happy, Momma!"* — Gabby age 3

The wrath of man crucified Jesus Christ, but the resurrection thwarted the intentions of man's heart of darkness. Paul writes, "Having disarmed the powers and authorities, he made a public spectacle of them, triumphing over them by the cross."[113] *Powers and authorities* refer to human institutions that leverage religion to control men's lives. Nevertheless, Jesus' resurrection proved that the spiritual authority and judgment wielded by man is merely a ruse. Not only could the grave not hold him, Jesus' death reconciled men to God. It is now obvious that there are now no intermediaries between God and man except the man, Jesus Christ.

The crucifixion paid the penalty for sin, and the resurrection is our hope. The resurrection is not the hope of "health and wealth" in this life but rather the hope of eternal life with Jesus Christ. Our hope is not temporal or present, but eternal. Paul says to the Corinthians, "If Christ has not been raised, our preaching is useless and so is your faith."[114] Our faith gains us nothing without the resurrection. However,

---

[113] Colossians 2:15 (NIV)
[114] 1 Corinthians 15:14 (NIV)

## Chapter 5

Christ has indeed been raised from the dead, the first-fruits of those who have fallen asleep. For since death came through a man, the resurrection of the dead comes also through a man. For as in Adam all die, so in Christ all will be made alive.[115]

On the cross, Jesus took our penalty. He became our sin and God judged him as sin. He gave up his life as a sacrifice for sin, and after three days in the tomb, God raised him up. Some people speculate about what happened during the three days that Jesus was dead; they come up with wild stories about how Jesus obtained salvation at the hand of the devil. Regardless of their morose spiritual fantasies, Scripture is not silent about the days between the crucifixion and the resurrection.

At Calvary, one thief mocked Jesus, but the other believed. Jesus told the believing thief, "I tell you the truth, today you will be with me in paradise." Peter tells us that after the crucifixion, Jesus was dead in the flesh, but alive in the spirit. During this time, Peter says, "[Jesus] went and preached to the spirits in prison who disobeyed long ago when God waited patiently in the days of Noah while the ark was being built."[116] Hebrews tells us, "[Jesus] entered the Most Holy Place once for all by his own blood, having obtained eternal redemption."[117]

The Romans crucified Jesus Thursday morning after an overnight trial. Early Thursday evening, before three stars were visible, Joseph of Arimathea and Nicodemus placed Jesus in the tomb. Thursday evening and Friday was the Passover Sabbath. Friday evening and Saturday was the regular Sabbath. Sunday, the third day, was resurrection day. In the interim period between the crucifixion and the resurrection, Jesus, as a high priest, offered his blood in the Most Holy Place in heaven; he met the thief (and other believers) in paradise; he preached to the souls killed in the great flood. Immediately upon Jesus' death, God was satisfied and the resurrection was secure. Although Jesus would spend three days and three nights in the heart of the earth (the grave), Matthew tells us that upon Jesus' death, "The veil of the temple was torn in two from top to bottom; and the earth shook and the rocks were split.

---

[115] 1 Corinthians 15:20-22 (NIV)
[116] 1Peter 3:19-20 (NIV)
[117] Hebrews 9:12 (NIV)

## The Resurrection

The tombs opened, and many bodies of the saints who had fallen asleep were raised."[118]

The veil symbolized the barrier that existed between God and man. At the sacrifice, the veil is torn, the barrier was removed; moreover, the dead are raised. There is nothing more needed to secure man's salvation. Jesus' resurrection is coming in three days, but redemption has been obtained.

Certainly, this is all mysterious to us and there are questions that we cannot answer, but we should not entertain speculation that is not consistent with what Scripture records. God ordained both Jesus' death and his resurrection. He ordained it, and he accomplished it. Because Jesus rose again, we also have hope of the resurrection. Nevertheless, death precedes resurrection. In fact, we are identified with Christ's death.

The Baptist liturgy during a baptism ceremony goes something like this: as the pastor lowers the convert into the water, he says, "Buried in the likeness of his death," and as he lifts the convert out of the water the pastor says, "Raised in the likeness of his resurrection." This is a paraphrase of Paul in Romans where Paul argues against continuing a sinful lifestyle. He says:

> What shall we say, then? Shall we go on sinning so that grace may increase? By no means! We died to sin, how can we live in it any longer? Or don't you know that **all of us who were baptized into Christ Jesus were baptized into his death**? **We were therefore buried with him through baptism into death** in order that, just as Christ was raised from the dead through the glory of the Father, we too may live a new life.[119]

Cara remembers her baptism even though she was very young. The heater in the baptismal was broken and the water was painfully cold. I stood there waist deep with the pastor. Cara was uncomfortable and afraid, but she was determined to obey Jesus.

Likewise, the choice to follow Jesus into his death can be frightening. In our salvation, we retrace the decisions of the fall of man. Instead of acting in pride and disobedience as Adam and Eve did, for salvation we choose humility and obedience unto death just as Jesus Christ did.

---

[118] Matthew 27:51-52 (NASB)
[119] Romans 6:1-4 (NIV)

# Chapter 5

Some days we fail. Paul anguished over his frailty. The good news is that Jesus has fulfilled all righteousness for us. It is not our righteousness that saves us, but his. We look forward to the resurrection when we will be whole like him and without our sinful natures. The requirements of the law are fulfilled, not by our works, but by his righteousness.

This brings up issues with legalism with which Christians continually struggle. Christians famously dictate what other Christians can and cannot do. Moral value has been assigned to smoking, drinking, movies, theatre, make-up, hairstyle, fashion, diet, exercise, body weight, musical style, church participation (attendance and financial support), political platforms, and just about everything imaginable. We sometimes presume that because we do not do certain things, we are better than someone who does them. Some Christians even write video games to teach their bigotry to a younger generation.

Legalism is hardly limited to Christianity. Islam is even more restrictive; does that make it more holy? Even godless organizations, such as PETA or Greenpeace, ascribe morality to actions. Such men establish various pseudo-moralities without acknowledging the righteous God who made them. Truly, the fundamental purpose of these self-aggrandizing mores is the manipulation of others. Self-righteousness comes in many sizes and colors, but true righteousness comes only by faith in Christ.

Judaism today obeys the Old Testament Law with various additions, deletions, and accommodations. Nevertheless, what value is the Law or legalism? To the Jew, the Law was required. It was part of the covenant between God and the people of Israel. It was not; however, part of the covenant between God and Abraham! This is an important point that few people acknowledge: Abraham was not under the Law of Moses, and God's promises to Abraham were not dependent upon Abraham or his descendants keeping the Law. Nevertheless, the Law of Moses is important. It reveals the righteousness of God, and it has blessed the world by serving as the basis of justice for all of Western Civilization.

At the giving of the Law, Moses brought down two stone tablets from Mount Sinai onto which God himself had carved the Ten Commandments. This, by the way, did not happen as Cecile B. DeMille depicted in the film version by the same title. Moses spent time on the mountain with the Creator

# The Resurrection

who looked like a man. This was one of many times in the Old Testament when God the Son appeared to man in a physical body. The Creator that had formed man from the dust of the ground now carves in stone a covenant between God and Israel. The two tablets were the two copies of the contract: God's copy and man's copy. Within the Ten Commandments were the rules for man's relationship to God, his family, and society. In other cultures, the law was simply, the king says . . . Now, for the Jews, the law is, "God spoke all these words:"

I am the LORD your God, who brought you out of Egypt, out of the land of slavery.

[1]You shall have no other gods before me.

[2]You shall not make for yourself an idol in the form of anything in heaven above or on the earth beneath or in the waters below. You shall not bow down to them or worship them; for I, the LORD your God, am a jealous God, punishing the children for the sin of the fathers to the third and fourth generation of those who hate me, but showing love to a thousand {generations} of those who love me and keep my commandments.

[3]You shall not misuse the name of the LORD your God, for the LORD will not hold anyone guiltless who misuses his name.

[4]Remember the Sabbath day by keeping it holy. Six days you shall labor and do all your work, but the seventh day is a Sabbath to the LORD your God. On it you shall not do any work, neither you, nor your son or daughter, nor your manservant or maidservant, nor your animals, nor the alien within your gates. For in six days the LORD made the heavens and the earth, the sea, and all that is in them, but he rested on the seventh day. Therefore the LORD blessed the Sabbath day and made it holy.

[5]Honor your father and your mother, so that you may live long in the land the LORD your God is giving you.

[6]You shall not murder.

[7]You shall not commit adultery.

[8]You shall not steal.

# Chapter 5

[9]You shall not give false testimony against your neighbor.

[10]You shall not covet your neighbor's house. You shall not covet your neighbor's wife, or his manservant or maidservant, his ox or donkey, or anything that belongs to your neighbor.[120]

Going forward from here, the law instructs the Jews how to offer sacrifices, how they are supposed to treat slaves, what they are to eat, personal hygiene, how they are to respect property, how they are to repay debts and injuries, and how they are to worship through giving. God commanded a law for just about every imaginable activity or behavior. Interestingly, God, as a matter of the Law, included the literalness of the six-day creation account, lest we begin to doubt the Genesis account.

The consequences for disobeying the law were severe. Many infractions incurred a death sentence. Other times, a sinner was ostracized. Thieves paid restitution: double the offense. If they could not repay their crimes, they were sold into slavery. The law required accountability for other people's property. You had to return lost livestock to its rightful owner regardless of whether it was convenient, even if the owner hated you or was your enemy; you still were obligated under the law to help. Obeying the law was not easy. It required diligence just to know what was required. Regarding the Law, even a non-Jew is held accountable according to his knowledge and his conscience. Paul says,

> All who sin apart from the law will also perish apart from the law, and all who sin under the law will be judged by the law. For it is not those who hear the law who are righteous in God's sight, but it is those who obey the law who will be declared righteous. (Indeed when Gentiles, who do not have the law, do by nature things required by the law, they are a law for themselves, even though they do not have the law, since they show that the requirements of the law are written on their hearts, their consciences also bearing witness, and their thoughts now accusing, now even defending them).[121]

---

[120] Exodus 20:1-17 (NIV)
[121] Romans 2:12-15 (NIV)

# The Resurrection

Paul says in Romans, "No one will be declared righteous in his sight by observing the law; rather, through the law we become conscious of sin."[122] The law informs our conscience, but it does not make us choose rightly. He also says, "The law was added so that the trespass might increase."[123] In other words, the law did not make men righteous; it only makes them more aware of their own unrighteousness. Moreover, he says, "The law was put in charge to lead us to Christ that we might be justified by faith. Now that faith has come, we are no longer under the supervision of the law."[124]

A question arises in the mind, how could we be under the law one day and no longer under the supervision of the law on the next? What happened? Did God change his mind? If he did not change his mind, then is the law still required? Paul writes,

**The law has authority over a man only as long as he lives**
. . . So, my brothers, you also died to the law through the body of
Christ, that you might belong to another, to him that was raised
from the dead, in order that we might bear fruit to God.[125]

Christians sometimes cherry-pick the Old Testament law. Churches teach tithing as being required, but ignore keeping the seventh day as a day of rest. Even if Christians set aside Sunday, as does the Westminster Catechism, as a holy day, it would violate the letter of the law because the first day of the week is not the seventh day. Nevertheless, if observation of the Sabbath is required, why would Paul say, "One man considers one day more sacred than another; another man considers every day alike. Each one should be fully convinced in his own mind."[126] Paul tells Titus that he should reprove the Cretans severely, "not paying attention to Jewish myths and commandments of men who turn away from the truth."[127] Legalism brings only bondage, and Paul commanded Titus to be harsh in his defense against legalism.

Paul tells the Galatians that by reverting to any part of the Law, they become obligated to fulfill all of the Law. In addition to keeping only part of the law, Christians famously make up their own laws. Paul summarizes them

---

[122] Romans 3:20 (NIV)
[123] Romans 5:20 (NIV)
[124] Galatians 3:24-25 (NIV)
[125] Romans 7:1b, 4 (NIV)
[126] Romans 14:5 (NIV)
[127] Titus 1:14 (NASB)

## Chapter 5

as, "Do not handle, do not taste, do not touch!"[128] He goes on to say that these made-up laws may seem wise but they have no value.

You might ask, what about ungodly behavior, is there nothing that is forbidden? Paul clarifies for the Galatians:

> The acts of the sinful nature are obvious: sexual immorality, impurity and debauchery; idolatry and witchcraft; hatred, discord, jealousy, fits of rage, selfish ambitions, dissensions, factions and envy, drunkenness, orgies, and the like. I warn you, as I did before, that those who live like this will not inherit the kingdom of God.[129]

Paul goes on to explain the contrast that is available to believers.

> But the fruit of the Spirit is love, joy, peace, patience, kindness, goodness, faithfulness, gentleness and self-control. Against such things there is no law. Those who belong to Christ Jesus have crucified the sinful nature with its passions and desires. Since we live by the Spirit, let us keep in step with the Spirit.[130]

Galatians 5:16 prefaces this discussion with, "Live by the Spirit and you will not gratify the desires of the sinful nature." Right behavior does not come from attention to a list of rules, but rather from a relationship with Jesus Christ. In other words if we are busy doing what the Spirit leads us to do, we will not be fulfilling our own selfish and sinful desires. After all, the behavior is not the goal, rather it is a byproduct of our relationship to Christ. Paul says,

> If Christ is in you, your body is dead because of sin, yet your spirit is alive because of righteousness. And if the Spirit of him who raised Jesus from the dead is living in you, he who raised Christ from the dead will also give life to your mortal bodies through his Spirit, who lives in you.[131]

Believers have died with Christ on the cross. God accepts Jesus' once-for-all sacrifice as a penalty for our sin. Just as God raised Jesus from the dead, we also are made alive to serve God. The law to which we were obligated, whether it was the Old Testament Law or the law of our own conscience, no longer condemns us not because we have no guilt before the law but because we have already died with Christ. Alive in Christ, we have the

---

[128] Colossians 2:21 (NASB)
[129] Galatians 5:19-21(NIV)
[130] Galatians 5:22-25(NIV)
[131] Romans 8:10-11 (NIV)

## The Resurrection

Spirit of God, and we now live by the Spirit, not by endless regulations. If we attempt to live under the law then we ignore the fact that we have died. If we live as though we have not died, then how is the power of the resurrection manifest in our lives? Legalism is opposed to resurrection because it focuses upon sustaining and reforming the dead flesh of our old nature.

This does not mean that we live without regard to sin or the consequences of our sin. Paul anguished that his sinful nature was still active within him. He wanted to do good because he had the Spirit, but he found himself still sinning. He explained that sin was not his true nature in Christ, but that sin still lived within him. He finally declares, "What a wretched man I am! Who will deliver me from the body of this death? Thanks be to God—through Jesus Christ our Lord!"[132]

For a time we, too, are trapped between what we know and want to do and what we find ourselves struggling against and doing nonetheless. Therefore, while we wrestle with sin within ourselves we also find ourselves incompatible with the world system. Jesus prays to the Father for those whom the Father has given to him, saying,

I have given them your word and the world has hated them, for
they are not of the world any more than I am of the world. My
prayer is not that you take them out of the world but that you
protect them from the evil one. They are not of the world, even as I
am not of it. Sanctify them by the truth; your word is truth. As you
sent me into the world, I have sent them into the world.[133]

Paul looked forward to the resurrection to answer and resolve the issue of sin, but until our physical resurrection, Jesus sends us into the world even as the Father sent him into the world. Until the resurrection, we are not isolated from the world even though the world hates us. Spiritually we live in Christ's resurrection, but in the flesh, we are still at war with our own bodies and at war with the world who hates us. Simply put, until the physical resurrection of the dead, we are not free of the influence of sin.

So when do we experience the resurrection? We experience the fullness of the resurrection when Christ returns. About this point, there is much confusion in Evangelical Christianity; nevertheless, Scripture is not

---

[132] Romans 7:24 (NIV)
[133] John 17:14-16 (NIV)

## Chapter 5

ambiguous regarding prophecies of Christ's return. At the time of Jesus' life on earth, the Jews were looking for a military and political savior. Many Old Testament prophecies looked forward to the coming of Messiah in power and glory, and these prophecies remain unfulfilled. When Christ comes again, he will come in power and glory.

Some Christians theorize that Christ's coming is divided into two appearances: the *rapture* of the church and Christ's return to set up his kingdom. Christians use the word *rapture* to describe our being gathered together to Christ in the sky. No event is named *The Rapture* in Scripture because Scripture does not differentiate between Jesus' coming to gather his saints and his coming in power and glory to set up his kingdom. Paul says,

> It is just for God to **repay with affliction those who afflict you, and** to **give relief to you who are afflicted** and to us as well **when the Lord Jesus will be revealed from heaven** with His mighty angels in flaming fire, dealing out retribution to those who do not know God and to those who do not obey the gospel of our Lord Jesus. **These will pay the penalty** of eternal destruction, away from the presence of the Lord and from the glory of his power, **when He comes to be glorified in His saints on that day**, and to be marveled at among all who have believed.[134]

This passage has some very long sentences, so it is hard to comprehend in a single reading all that it means. The bolded text assembled into a paraphrase says, "The Lord Jesus will repay with affliction those who afflict you and give relief to you who are afflicted when he is revealed from heaven. Those who do not obey the gospel will pay the penalty when he comes to be glorified in his saints on that day." From these verses, we see two purposes in his coming: glory and judgment or retribution. Nevertheless, this passage does not indicate two comings, but one.

Looking back at the entire verse, we notice that "the Lord Jesus will be revealed from heaven with His mighty angels." We can compare this to Jesus' account of his return:

> Then the sign of the Son of Man will appear in the sky, and then all the tribes of the earth will mourn, and they will see the SON OF MAN COMING ON THE CLOUDS OF THE SKY with power and

---
[134] 2 Thessalonians 1:6-10 (NASB)

## The Resurrection

great glory. And He will send forth His angels with a GREAT TRUMPET and THEY WILL GATHER TOGETHER His elect from the four winds, from one end of the sky to the other."[135]

Now these verses are full of details, too, but what we need to see is that both 2 Thessalonians 1 and Matthew 24 deal with the Lord's return. We can see that what Paul writes about Christ's return, "[He] will be revealed from heaven with His mighty angels," is similar to what Jesus himself says about the coming of his kingdom in Matthew 24, "they will see the SON OF MAN COMING ON THE CLOUDS OF THE SKY with power and great glory. And He will send forth His angels . . ."

Paul presents no distinction between Christ coming to be glorified in his saints and his coming to punish the unbelieving. Furthermore, Paul tells the Thessalonians, do not be deceived by any false teaching about the Lord's return, because he says, "*it will not come* [until] the apostasy comes first, and the man of lawlessness is revealed." He goes on to describe the revelation of the man of lawlessness saying, "he takes his seat in the temple of God, displaying himself as being God."[136] John calls this person *antichrist* in his letters, in Revelation, after seeing his wickedness first hand, John calls him *the beast*.

Paul says that the Lord Jesus Christ will not return until the man of lawlessness is revealed, but what did Jesus say about the timing of his return? He said, "Therefore **when you see the ABOMINATION OF DESOLATION** which was spoken through Daniel the prophet, **standing in the holy place** (let the reader understand), then those who are in Judea must flee to the mountains."[137] Now this is speculation, but what would be more abominable than the Antichrist in the temple of God declaring himself to be God? What man would be more lawless than one standing in the temple of God declaring himself to be God? Paul and Jesus seem to be referring to the same prophetic event. Jesus goes on to say, "For **then there will be a great tribulation**, such as has not occurred since the beginning of the world until now, nor ever will."

Paul talked about the man of lawlessness standing in the temple of God claiming to be God, and Jesus talked about the Abomination of Desolation

---

[135] Matthew 24:30-31 (NASB)
[136] 2 Thessalonians 2:3-6 (NASB)
[137] Matthew 24:15-16 (NASB)

happening in the holy place of the temple. Jesus says that after this event the Great Tribulation will come. Jesus is clear; it is not just a time of tribulation, it is a time worse than the world has ever seen and worse than the world will ever see again. The tribulation, or affliction, happens after the Abomination of Desolation (the revelation of the man of lawlessness). Paul says this must occur before the Lord Jesus returns, but what does Jesus say?

Immediately after the tribulation of those days . . .[138]

- THE SUN WILL BE DARKENED,
- AND THE MOON WILL NOT GIVE ITS LIGHT,
- AND THE STARS WILL FALL from the sky,
- And the powers of the heavens will be shaken.
- And then the sign of the Son of Man will appear in the sky,
- And then all the tribes of the earth will mourn,
- And they will see the SON OF MAN COMING ON THE CLOUDS OF THE SKY with power and great glory
- And He will send forth His angels with A GREAT TRUMPET
- And THEY WILL GATHER TOGETHER His elect from the four winds, from one end of the sky to the other.

So according to Jesus, his return will follow the Great Tribulation, which follows the Abomination of Desolation. Matthew 24 agrees with 2 Thessalonians, or rather 2 Thessalonians agrees with Matthew 24. Paul tells us that the return of Christ also corresponds to the resurrection of the dead. He writes,

> We do not want you to be uninformed, brethren, about those who are asleep, so that you will not grieve as do the rest who have no hope. For if we believe that Jesus died and rose again, even so God will bring with Him those who have fallen asleep in Jesus. For this we say to you by the word of the Lord, that we who are alive and remain until the coming of the Lord, will not precede those who have fallen asleep.
>
> For the Lord Himself will descend from heaven with a shout, with the voice of the archangel and with the trumpet of God, and the dead in Christ will rise first. Then **we who are alive and remain**

---

[138] Matthew 24:29-31 (NASB)

# The Resurrection

**will be caught up together with them in the clouds to meet the Lord in the air**, and so we shall always be with the Lord.[139]

Those who are dead will return with Christ and will be resurrected. Those of us who might remain will be caught up in the sky to meet the Lord. Paul's description is consistent with Jesus' own description of his coming in Matthew 24. Paul reveals other details about the resurrection to the Corinthians,

> Behold, I tell you a mystery; we will not all sleep, but **we will all be changed,** in a moment, in the twinkling of an eye, **at the last trumpet**; for the trumpet will sound, and the dead will be raised imperishable, and we will be changed. For this perishable must put on the imperishable, and this mortal must put on immortality. But when this perishable will have put on the imperishable, and this mortal will have put on immortality, then will come about the saying that is written,
> 
> > "DEATH IS SWALLOWED UP in victory.
> > O DEATH, WHERE IS YOUR VICTORY?
> > O DEATH, WHERE IS YOUR STING?"
> 
> The sting of death is sin, and the power of sin is the law, but thanks be to God, who gives us the victory through our Lord Jesus Christ.[140]

The resurrection is more than just coming back to life. Jesus raised Lazarus and others from the dead but they still awaited this transformation. The physical resurrection we anticipate is more glorious because God transforms us into imperishable, immortal, living beings that are victorious over sin and death through the work of Jesus Christ. In 1 Corinthians 15 Paul does not mention being caught up in the clouds, but he indicates that this resurrection transformation occurs at the *last trumpet*. The trumpet in 1 Corinthians 15 ties together with the trumpet Matthew 24 and the trumpet in 1 Thessalonians 4. Remember that Paul calls this the *last trumpet*.

We could delve deeply into the books of Daniel, Ezekiel, Zechariah, and Revelation, extract every reference to the Lord's return, and compare them, but that is beyond the scope of our discussion. What we would learn,

---

[139] 1 Thessalonians 4:13-17 (NASB)
[140] 1 Corinthians 15:51-57 (NASB)

however, is that Scripture does not include the noun *Rapture* in its vocabulary. The verb *harpazo* is used to convey many things from being arrested to being caught up to meet the Lord. When it talks about our being *caught up* to meet Christ, it says that this occurs at his *coming*. When it talks about God's wrath against the nations, we discover that it happens at Christ's *coming*. 2 Thessalonians 1 ties his coming for his elect and his coming in wrath together into one coming. Revelation 20 calls Jesus' coming for his church the *first resurrection*.

You might ask, What about the "thief in the night," from Matthew 24 and 1 Thessalonians 5? Does this not mean that Christ could return at any moment? If you look at Revelation 16:15, however, Jesus says, "Behold, I come like a thief! Blessed is he who stays awake and keeps his clothes with him, so that he may not go naked and be shamefully exposed."[141] Look closely at the context of Revelation 16:15. Jesus gives this warning between the sixth and seventh bowl of God's wrath during the tribulation. Jesus warns the saints to be ready for his return immediately before the last bowl of wrath. Remember what Jesus prayed. He told the Father, "**My prayer is not that you take them out of the world** but that you protect them from the evil one." Scripture appears to teach that the *world* will not know when Christ will return. God, on the other hand, has given to believers signs for which to watch including the Abomination of Desolation, the Great Tribulation, and finally the gathering of the armies of the world at Armageddon. We cannot predict the date when this will happen, but he tells us to recognize it when we see it and to be ready.

At the last bowl of wrath, a loud voice comes from the throne of God, saying, "It is done." This corresponds to the seventh trumpet in Revelation 11 where loud voices in heaven sing out,

> The kingdom of this world
> has become the kingdom of our Lord
> and of his Christ,
> and he will reign forever and ever.[142]

John refers to the *seventh trumpet*. Paul refers to the *last trumpet*. At the last trumpet, the dead are raised and all believers from all generations receive

---
[141] Revelation 16:15 (NIV)
[142] Revelation 11:15 (NASB)

## The Resurrection

their new imperishable, immortal bodies. The church, the bride of Christ, is caught up to meet the bridegroom at his coming (Matthew 25:6). If the church is *raptured* at the last trumpet, but Jesus comes to set up his kingdom later at the seventh trumpet after the pouring out of God's wrath, then it is fair to ask, *how many trumpets will sound after the last trumpet?* Scripture has many writers, but only one Author, so again we ask *how many trumpets after the last one?*

Some disagree with the timing presented in Scripture. They believe they have *new* revelation indicating an early exit of the church. This teaching emerged about 200 years ago and has infiltrated many Evangelical denominations. Their logic distorts Scripture and they play vocabulary shell games using terms like *dispensation, rapture* (as a noun), and *second coming*; none of which are found in Scripture, but are still necessary to support their doctrines.

Dispensational theology divides the earth's spiritual history into dispensations. It seeks to demonstrate that God responded differently to man in each dispensation. Some believe that when the dispensation of the church age ends, then God must rapture the church. Romans chapter 11 reveals that the Gentiles' domination of the church will end, but that does not necessitate *rapture*.

Jesus told the Pharisees, "The kingdom of God will be taken away from you and given to a people producing the fruit of it."[143] In this, he prophesied the age of the Gentiles; however, since the first century the Jews have remained on earth, even though the Gospel of the Kingdom is now preached by Gentiles. If God grafts the natural branch back into the olive tree (Romans 11:24), it does not mean that the church is raptured. Rather it means that Jewish believers will once again be the champions of the Gospel! Revelation 7 talks about 144,000 such missionaries.

Certainly, Israel is temporarily blinded so that the Gospel can come to the non-Jewish world, but even today there is a remnant of believing Jews. While God revealed himself at different times and in different ways throughout history, there are only two covenants: the *Old Covenant* and the *New Covenant*. The difference between them is that the old existed before Christ and anticipated his coming, and the new was revealed in Christ and

---

[143] Matthew 21:43 (NASB)

anticipates his coming again. You might say the old is older and the new is newer. Christ is the focus of both covenants, and within both covenants, salvation comes by grace through faith. Hebrews 11:4 emphasizes that even Abel, the second son of Adam, was justified by faith.

Although the Law of Moses advised man's conscience, both law and conscience are incapable of creating righteousness. God only accepts our faith, not our works. Therefore, as much as things have changed throughout history, God's requirements have remained the same. He requires faith.

When confronted with dispensational theology realize that man, not God, defined the system. Theological systems contain some truth, but men use them to distort truth as well. The application of a human theory cannot dictate our interpretation of Scripture; otherwise, we might practice *circulus in probando*, or circular reasoning using theories to interpret Scripture and then using the interpreted Scripture to support the theories.

In computer programming, a circular reference results in a *stack overflow* wherein code cannot stop executing until it errs after consuming all the memory in the stack. While computers reject circular reasoning, theologians often embrace it. Actually, when confronted with their false logic, theologians can overflow their stack as well. Meanwhile we should search Scripture to make sure that what we think it says is consistent within the passage and within the collection of Scripture as a whole.

Even though Jesus said that he will come and his angels "WILL GATHER TOGETHER His elect from the four winds . . . *after the tribulation of those days*," many theologians disagree. According to them, the rapture is a sort of *fly by* that portends God's wrath, but does not follow it. This is not consistent with Paul's message to the Thessalonians or Jesus' words in Matthew 24. Read for yourselves.

Nevertheless, there are three basic schools of thought on the *rapture:* the pre-tribulation, mid-tribulation, and pre-wrath rapture. They are all the same in this regard: they believe that the God must *rapture* the church because he will not pour wrath upon his church. This seems like a rational argument, but upon a closer look, it is like saying, *if it rains, I will get wet, and therefore it will not rain*. While we might get wet when it rains, we will not get wet if we stay within a shelter. Others might get wet when we do not. We might see other people soaked with rain even as we drive by comfortably

## The Resurrection

dry. Likewise, it is illogical to say, *if God's wrath is poured out upon the earth, I will suffer from God's wrath, therefore God's wrath will not be poured out upon the earth until after I fly away.*

Although believers will not incur God's wrath, we will witness it if we remain alive until the Lord comes. The coming of wrath does not mean that believers will suffer from it. Noah waited in the ark until the waters of wrath subsided. The waters that buried the earth also lifted Noah and his family to safety. Noah received mercy by faith, but he also witnessed God's wrath destroying the world.

Habakkuk says of the end days, "the righteous will live by his faith"[144] and so it is with us, and so it should be in the midst of extreme trial and every day. Each day presents an opportunity to walk in faith and more so as the culture decays into godlessness. If we cannot be faithful today, then how will we be faithful in the midst of a great trial? If we do not trust God now, how will we find the faith to trust him when armies are coming to destroy us and the earth is disintegrating beneath our feet?

Regardless of when Christ comes in glory, we must be ready and remain faithful because we do not know when we will go to be with him. Even if we knew the exact moment in time that Christ would return, we would still not know what hour he has appointed for us. As we see the world decaying into sin, we must put on the righteousness that is by faith. Remember Solomon's warning? "Remember him—before . . . dust returns to the ground it came from and the spirit returns to God who gave it."

We know that Jesus Christ will return in power and glory. We know that he will bring with him the souls of the dead. We know that the dead will be resurrected, and those that are living will be transformed. We look forward to some exciting stuff. Nevertheless, do we know when our lives on earth will end? Will we remember him? When our time on earth ends, will he find us faithful?

The resurrection burned in Paul's heart. He lived for the resurrection with such passion that he would have gladly died for it. To the Philippians he wrote of his ambitions, saying,

> Whatever things were gain to me, those things I have counted as loss for the sake of Christ. More than that, I count all things to be

---

[144] Habakkuk 2:4 (NASB)

loss in view of the surpassing value of knowing Christ Jesus my Lord, for whom I have suffered the loss of all things, and count them but rubbish so that I may gain Christ, and may be found in Him, not having a righteousness of my own derived from the Law, but that which is through faith in Christ, the righteousness which comes from God on the basis of faith, **that I may know Him and the power of His resurrection and the fellowship of His sufferings, being conformed to His death; in order that I may attain to the resurrection of the dead.**[145]

Paul, writing to Timothy about God's faithfulness to believers, says,

Therefore I endure everything for the sake of the elect, that they too may obtain the salvation that is in Christ Jesus, with eternal glory [resurrection].

Here is a trustworthy saying:
If we died with him, we will also live with him;
If we endure, we will also reign with him.
If we disown him, he will disown us;
If we are faithless, he will remain faithful,
For he cannot disown himself.[146]

That is our hope, the hope of the resurrection. Because we died with him at the cross, we will live with him in eternity. If we endure in this life, we will reign with him in the next life, and even when we are faithless; he remains faithful because he is faithful to his own name.

Because we have the hope of the resurrection, our lives can be different. We can struggle with our weaknesses and know that our sinful bodies, sown in weakness, will be raised incorruptible in power and glory. Struggling with our weakness is not following the Law, it is grasping for faith just as the father of a demonized boy in Mark cried out to Jesus, "I do believe, help me overcome my unbelief."[147] It was an honest assessment of where he stood and where he knew he needed to be. We, too, need to be honest and say, "Lord, help my unbelief!"

---

[145] Philippians 3:7-11 (NASB)
[146] 2 Timothy 2:10-13 (NIV)
[147] Mark 9:24 (NIV)

## The Resurrection

Paul says of the resurrection, "Then we shall see face to face. Now I know in part; then I shall know fully, even as I am fully known."[148] We can look today at the desperate culture, and we can know that Jesus will someday rule and everything will be made right. We can look at our own frailty and know by faith that Christ can and will be glorified in us. We cannot completely understand it, but we can cling to it by faith.

In Revelation 21, John hears a voice coming from the throne of God,

> Now the dwelling of God is with men,
> and he will live with them.
> They will be his people,
> and God himself will be with them
> and be their God.
> He will wipe away every tear from their eyes.
> There will be no more death
> or mourning or crying or pain,
> for the old order of things
> has passed away. [149]

In the new earth, God's throne will reside within New Jerusalem. God who has previously maintained his throne in heaven will now dwell among men! This is a change to the order of eternity! We do not go to heaven for eternity; God himself comes to earth. There will be no barriers between God and his people. God will fulfill all the needs of our hearts. God himself will wipe the tears from our eyes. This is the eternal hope that we have.

This is the Resurrection.

---

[148] 1 Corinthians 13:12 (NIV)
[149] Revelation 21:3-4 (NIV)

# CHAPTER 6—THE WRATH OF GOD

*"Haughhhhhhht!"* — Gabby age 1
*"I'd rweally rwather be in Minnesota where it's chillwie"* — Gabby age 3

On the cross, Jesus endured the wrath of man, so that man could escape the wrath of God. While Jesus' suffering revealed the malice of man toward his Creator, the greatest pain that Christ endured was not the nails, thorns, or beatings. When the sins of the world were put upon Jesus Christ, his communion with the Father was interrupted. God's favor turned away as Jesus endured the judgment for sin, that is, death. We cannot understand the degree of Christ's anguish at this moment. He cried out, "My God, My God, why have you forsaken me?" The psalmist prophetically wrote those words in Psalm 22. The psalmist's words echo the deepest human despair, and so as he cried out *"Eloi, Eloi, lama sabachthani,"* Christ despaired more than any man ever did; more accurately he despaired more than all men. The pain inflicted on his body, soul, and spirit by this separation and rejection by the Father was as great as all the human suffering in the entire world from all ages because it carried within it all the human suffering from all the ages. He bore the consequence for man's sin to spare us from the winepress of God's wrath.

In modern Christianity, there is needless debate about the nature and extent of God's wrath. Many modern theologians trivialize the wrath of God. They reason that God would not punish man too severely: not so severely as condemning someone to eternal torment. This opinion stems mainly from

## Chapter 6

man's attempt to cast God in man's image. Man has always sought a more human God: someone with more understanding. This, of course, is silliness. Jesus, who is Creator God, became a man and was tempted as a man only without sin. After living a sinless life, he became our sin for the purpose of judgment. Not only does he know us because he created us; he knows us because he became a man and because he took upon his human body all our sin. Nevertheless, people still try to manufacture a kinder, gentler God.

Such speculation cannot define God; rather it reveals the hardness of man's heart and his extreme animosity toward his Creator because God, as he says he is, is not acceptable to his creation. Scripture, however, is clear regarding both the certainty and nature of God's wrath. Because of sin, mankind is under the wrath of God; however, through faith in Jesus Christ we have no fear of God's wrath. Rather his wrath against those who do not believe reveals the extent of his grace and mercy toward believers. Minimizing or dismissing the wrath of God also minimizes or dismisses Christ's work on Calvary. From the beginning of the New Testament, the wrath of God is central to the doctrine of salvation.

Before Jesus began his public ministry, John the Baptist came preaching, "Repent for the kingdom of heaven is at hand." What is it about the kingdom of heaven that would cause people to want or need to repent? We understand better when we realize who was calling men to repentance. Who was the man, John the Baptist?

John is unique in the cast of New Testament characters for a number of reasons. He was an odd personality; he dressed in a camel's hair robe or tunic fastened by a leather belt. He ate locust and wild honey. He was a wild man to say the least. We might compare him to someone today wandering downtown in tattered clothes with unkempt hair wearing a sandwich board declaring, "REPENT, THE END IS NEAR." Nevertheless, John was no lunatic; he was a prophet. Nor was he just any prophet, he was one who was promised by the Old Testament prophets Isaiah and Malachi. John the Baptist was a prophet of great stature.

John was Jesus' cousin. John's parents, Zacharias and Elizabeth were both of the tribe of Levi, descendants of Aaron the high priest. Mary, the mother of Jesus, was of the tribe of Judah and a descendant of David.

# The Wrath of God

Nevertheless, Mary and Elizabeth were cousins; perhaps their mothers were sisters.

The angel Gabriel announced the birth of John to his father, Zacharias, while Zacharias was serving as a priest in the temple in Jerusalem. In announcing the birth of John, Gabriel quoted the prophet Malachi and the closing verses of the Old Testament, saying,

> It is he who will go as a forerunner before Him in the spirit and power of Elijah, TO TURN THE HEARTS OF THE FATHERS BACK TO THE CHILDREN, and the disobedient to the attitude of the righteous, so as to make ready a people prepared for the Lord.[150]

John was full of the Holy Spirit even while he was in his mother's womb. Mary came to visit Elizabeth having just conceived Jesus by the Holy Spirit. When Mary entered the house and called to Elizabeth, John leaped for joy inside his mother's belly. As an adult, John was fully aware of his calling. When asked by the religious Jews to tell them who he was, he answered, "I am A VOICE OF ONE CRYING IN THE WILDERNESS, 'MAKE STRAIGHT THE WAY OF THE LORD,' as Isaiah the prophet said."[151] When he said this, he was quoting Isaiah 40:3.

Although John came in the spirit and power of Elijah, he never performed any miraculous sign (John 10:41, if you are curious). John's prophetic power, the spirit and power of Elijah, was manifest exclusively in the message he proclaimed beginning with, "Repent, for the kingdom of heaven is at hand."

Jesus' own testimony of John the Baptist was this, "This is the one about whom it is written, 'BEHOLD, I SEND MY MESSENGER AHEAD OF YOU, WHO WILL PREPARE YOUR WAY BEFORE YOU,'"[152] Jesus was quoting Malachi 3:1 and the promise of one who would precede the coming of the day of the Lord. Malachi, as the last book in the Old Testament Scripture, looked forward to the ultimate salvation of Israel. Jesus tells people that John was the one who had come before the Savior. Privately Jesus told his disciples in Matthew 11 and 17 that John was the fulfillment of the final prophecy of the Old Testament, "Behold, I am going to send you Elijah the prophet before the

---

[150] Luke 1:17 (NASB)
[151] John 1:23 (NASB)
[152] Luke 7:27 (NASB)

coming of the great and terrible day of the Lord."[153] Jesus also said, "Among those born of women there has not risen anyone greater than John the Baptist."[154] This does not mean that John was greater than all the Old Testament prophets; it only means that all the Old Testament prophets were not greater than John. John the Baptist was, in fact, the culmination of all the Old Testament prophets.

John's message, as the apex of all the Old Testament prophets, was the baptism of repentance for the forgiveness of sins. Now John's message did not come from within himself. Baptism was not his idea. His message came from the Holy Spirit, but his message was unusual. Baptism was not foreign to the Jews of John's days, but John's baptism was distinctive. There were ceremonial cleansings, and there was the baptism of proselytes, or non-Jewish converts, but the baptism of repentance that John taught was a new concept to the Jews. Baptism of repentance for the forgiveness of sin challenged the Jews' belief about salvation.

John's message was a message of salvation by faith and judgment for the unbelieving. The Pharisees' confidence was in Abraham and their relationship to Abraham rather than in God and their relationship to him. The Pharisees acted as if God owed them something because of who they were, because of their birthright in Abraham. When John saw that the Pharisees and Sadducees were also coming to him for baptism, he challenged them asking, "Who warned you to flee from the wrath to come? Therefore bear fruit in keeping with repentance."[155] Baptism without repentance was meaningless for salvation. It also slandered John's message.

From John's response to the Jews, we learn that the purpose of repentance was to escape wrath. We also learn that repentance includes a change of attitude. John was not eager to baptize those who were not repentant; it would only muddle his message. John's message was also more complex than merely salvation through immersion in the Jordan River. The baptism of repentance was a way of preparing the heart for the coming of the Christ. Paul explained the baptism of John to the Ephesians this way, "John baptized with the baptism of repentance, telling the people to believe in Him

---

[153] Malachi 4:5 (NASB)
[154] Matthew 11:11 (NASB)
[155] Matthew 3:7-8 (NASB)

# The Wrath of God

who was coming after him, that is, in Jesus."[156] The baptism of repentance prepared the heart of the baptized to believe in Jesus Christ. Baptism without belief was ineffective. This heartfelt repentance, expressed outwardly by water baptism, would spare the baptized from the wrath of God that was coming. Throughout Scripture, salvation always comes by faith and John's baptism is no different. Baptism by John expressed the faith of those baptized.

While John's ministry prepared hearts to believe in Jesus Christ, John's own expectation of Jesus' coming was the great and terrible day of the Lord. John was expecting that the coming of Jesus Christ would also reveal the wrath of God against the disobedient and unbelieving. We learn in Luke 7 that John sent messengers to ask Jesus whether he was indeed the Christ to whom Jesus quoted Old Testament prophecies that would reassure John.

Although John's expectation was the day of wrath, John's own prophecy about Jesus indicated the purpose of Jesus' incarnation. After Jesus' baptism by John and after Jesus' temptation in the desert, John saw Jesus walking toward him and he cried out, "Behold, the Lamb of God who takes away the sin of the world."[157] Although John's expectation was a Christ coming in power and glory rendering wrath against the unbelieving, he prophesied regarding the sacrificial death of Jesus Christ.

As John's ministry was declining and Jesus' ministry was beginning, Jesus' disciples baptized people also. When John's disciples asked him about Jesus' growing popularity, he gave them what was essentially a beautiful and eloquent resignation and good-bye speech. This is much more than an old-soldiers-never-die farewell. Being fully aware of his position and purpose, John compares Jesus to the bridegroom and himself to the one who stands with the bridegroom. He says, "So this joy of mine has been made full. He must increase and I must decrease." Then John gives his final message, the culmination of his life and ministry; he says, "He who believes in the Son has eternal life; but he who does not obey the Son will not see life, but the wrath of God abides on him."[158] So the final prophecy from the final *Old Testament* prophet of whom there was no one greater indicates two outcomes for man: either eternal life in the Son or the abiding wrath of God.

---

[156] Acts 19:4 (NASB)
[157] John 1:29 (NASB)
[158] John 3:36 (NASB)

# Chapter 6

John's expectation to see the wrath of God revealed in power by the person of Jesus Christ has not materialized, but he understands that although the wrath of God has not been revealed it still rests upon the unbelieving. John has done all that he can do to prepare hearts to receive the Christ, now each man lives or dies based on his faithfulness to the Son of God. The wrath of God still abides even if the coming of the Son did not yet fulfill John's expectations. We now know that the judgment that John was expecting will follow Christ's coming that he prophesied in Matthew 24.

Nevertheless, what is the wrath that abides upon the unbelieving? John, the Apostle, who wrote about John the Baptist in the Gospel of John, also gives us a glimpse of the wrath of God coming with the return of Jesus Christ. John writes in Revelation,

> Then another angel, a third one, followed them, saying with a loud voice, "If anyone worships the beast and his image, and receives a mark on his forehead or on his hand, he also will drink of the wine of the wrath of God; which is mixed in full strength in the cup of His anger; and he will be tormented with fire and brimstone in the presence of the holy angels and the presence of the Lamb. And the smoke of their torment goes up forever and ever; they have no rest day and night, those who worship the beast and his image, and whoever receives the mark of his name."[159]

For anyone to deny that the Scripture teaches eternal punishment, he would have to dismiss this passage, and we will not entertain arguments in this regard in any detail. Nevertheless, some claim that the eternal nature of this punishment only applies to those who receive the mark of the beast as detailed in Revelation 13. Others presumably receive a lesser degree of judgment. This interpretation requires some imagination on the part of the reader; moreover, it is silly conjecture to think that some measure of wrath would be more or less preferable to another measure of wrath. Should some expect *Wrath-Lite* instead, with 30 percent less torment than God's regular wrath? If someone actually experienced wrath, but *less* wrath, would he have a frame of reference to appreciate that fact? Would he be grateful? God's wrath is full strength and delivered without reservation to those who disobey, just as his mercy is complete and fully effective for those who believe.

---

[159] Revelation 14:9-11 (NASB)

## The Wrath of God

What the angel is telling John in this passage is that the unavoidable consequence of receiving the mark of the beast, or worshiping the beast and his image, is the eternal wrath of God. People who reject God fully and completely cannot later turn to repentance. Jesus likewise in Matthew 12:41 said blaspheming the Holy Spirit cannot be forgiven. He was speaking to those who had witnessed the power of God through the ministry of Jesus Christ, but had attributed the Holy Spirit's power to Satan. For these there was no possibility of repentance because they had seen all the evidence they needed to know Jesus was the Christ, but chose to reject him anyway. Hebrews 6 says of those who turn away after tasting the "good word of God . . . It is impossible to renew them again to repentance."[160] From these passages, we see that there are people who are beyond the grace of God because they have deliberately rejected it.

Hebrews offers Esau as an illustration of such a person, "He found no place for repentance, though he sought for it with tears."[161] Esau is a particularly sobering example because he reveals that remorsefulness and repentance are not equivalent. Esau was remorseful but he found no room for repentance. Many false religions teach remorsefulness, but true repentance, repentance that is acceptable to God, puts hope for redemption in the work of Jesus Christ alone. During the tribulation, when people worship the Antichrist there will be no avenue for repentance available to them. This is not a new or more severe punishment; rather it is consistent with the way God has dealt with those who have rejected him outright throughout the ages.

The wrath of God awaits the unrepentant, not because of their degree of wickedness, but because they do not believe. Jesus proclaims in his comparison of the sheep and the goats, "Then he will say to those on his left hand, 'Depart from me, you who are cursed, into the eternal fire prepared for the devil and his angels." Jesus says, "These will go away into eternal punishment, but the righteous into eternal life." [162] It is interesting to notice in Matthew 25 that the ones who are sent off into eternal punishment are those whose faith is empty. Those who are cursed are those who have confidence in their own works for salvation. They are religious, but they lack compassion for their fellow man. They have never experienced life-

---

[160] Hebrews 6:5-6 (NASB)
[161] Hebrews 12:17 (NASB)
[162] Matthew 25:41, 46 (NASB)

transforming faith and God will judge them regardless of their apparent religiousness.

Some have argued that *eternal punishment* in Matthew 25 does not mean eternal in the simple sense of the word; they suppose that it does not mean never ending but something else such as *extreme*. Nevertheless, the same word describes *eternal life* that is used to describe *eternal punishment*. Literally, it says, "punishment of the ages" and "life of the ages." If we would say that there is no *eternal punishment*, no punishment enduring for the ages, then we would also have to declare that there is no *eternal life*. Others suppose that the wrath of God causes annihilation and ceasing to exist is eternal in nature, but not severe. This opinion ignores the angel's description of God's wrath expressed in Revelation, "the smoke of their torment goes up forever and ever; they have no rest day and night."[163]

From a perspective of parsimony, Scripture is clear that the wrath of God will punish the unbeliever forever; the suffering will be real, extreme, and eternal. Scripture does not support erstwhile opinions. Nevertheless, some distort or ignore Scripture to assert what they want to believe regardless of what Scripture teaches.

In Revelation 19 and 20 we see that the beast and the false prophet and Satan are thrown into the lake of fire as well as all the dead whose names are not written in the Book of Life. The fate of all who do not believe in the Son of God is the same: they "will be tormented day and night forever and ever."[164] This is the extent and nature of the wrath of God revealed against men and angels who rebel. This is the wrath that we all are worthy of receiving by virtue of both Adam's sin and our own, and this is the wrath that we escape by faith in Jesus Christ.

Many within modern Christianity doubt the eternality of punishment or believe that God lacks the resolve to condemn men to the lake of fire. They compose rational arguments, but their logic has one central fault: they allow man to define who God is, rather than believing God's testimony about himself.

Paul preempts the Romans from making such rational arguments about God. He asks, "Who are you, O man, who answers back to God? The thing

---
[163] Revelation 14:11 (NASB)
[164] Revelation 20:10 (NASB)

# The Wrath of God

molded will not say to the molder, 'Why did you make me like this,' will it?"[165] Paul is telling the Romans that they do not have to understand God, but he is also telling them that God will not justify himself to man. What we think or understand are irrelevant to the truth. God is who he is and will do as he wills.

A popular misconception among those who *do* believe in eternal punishment is the notion that the devil and his demons torment unbelievers for eternity. Some people suppose that damnation results when God fails to rescue us from the clutches of Satan; man must respond to God in order to save himself from the devil. This is ridiculous. It is saying that God and Satan divvy up the reward of men's souls based on men's own personal choices. In this regard it puts the devil on equal footing with God as if there are two Gods of eternity: one of mercy another of wrath; one light and one dark; one Yin and one Yang.

Nevertheless, even Satan is a created being whom God will hold accountable in judgment. Satan gains nothing from the deception he perpetrates. Nor does God lose anything from those who reject him; as Paul proclaims, "So then He has mercy on whom He desires, and He hardens whom he desires."[166] This is the way it is and the way it must be, for if it were any other way God would be diminished and another's will would become sovereign. Some are destined to salvation while others are destined to wrath.

Those chosen for salvation respond in faith to the message of atoning work of Jesus Christ while the others destined for wrath, reject the Gospel message in unbelief. In this way, while God's will prevails man still experiences freewill. Freewill is simply behaving consistently with our nature. Scientists tell us that we experience freewill *after* our brains have committed to their decisions. We make decisions based upon who we are, and not upon our ability to reason (although our reasoning often justifies our actions). Therein we experience freewill even though our actions are determinate.

God rejects no one responding in faith to the Gospel. However, those rejecting his salvation endure his wrath according to his will. Those of us who are saved are humbled when we realize that even the faith which brought us to salvation did not come from within ourselves, but rather was the gift of

---
[165] Romans 9:20 (NASB)
[166] Romans 9:18 (NASB)

# Chapter 6

God (Ephesians 2:8, 9). If God did not intervene, our freewill would choose wrongly. Paul quotes Psalm 53 when he explains that we cannot choose salvation apart from God's intervention. He says,

> There is no one righteous,
> Not even one.
> There is no one who understands,
> No one who seeks God.[167]

While all of these truths are still shrouded in mystery, we know that they are true because of who God is, and all things exist for him and for his purposes. He is the only one who can create. He is the only one who can save. Anything that attempts to exist without him is unrighteousness, and all unrighteousness will return to him to meet his righteous judgment. This judgment is fulfilled either by the atoning judgment of sin in the body of Jesus Christ at the cross or by the full measure of God's wrath against the unrepentant and unbelieving in the eternal flames of the lake of fire.

Those of us who believe will not encounter the wrath of God because he has provided for us a way to escape. Instead of the wrath of God, we can experience the love of God. John writes, "This is love: not that we loved God, but that he loved us and sent his Son as an atoning sacrifice for our sins."[168] The love that he showed us not only spares us from wrath but also makes us his children and joint heirs with Jesus Christ. Knowing that we exist for God we can reject the lies that would seduce us to live for ourselves. This we do, not to secure our salvation, but because our salvation is secure.

There are many questions we can have regarding the fate of unbelievers who have not heard the Gospel. Scripture does not address this directly and for good cause: God will not justify himself to man. We know that Jesus preached to the souls who perished in the flood. One thief on the cross came to repentance in his final moments of life. We know that David upon the loss of an infant son said, "I will go to him, but he will not return to me."[169] What do these things mean? We can speculate as much as we want, but the truth is that eventually, regardless of our speculation, we must trust the Creator to do what is right with his creation. God does what is right, not based on some

---

[167] Romans 3:10-11 (NIV)
[168] 1 John 4:10 (NIV)
[169] 2 Samuel 12:23 (NASB)

# The Wrath of God

external standard that we define, but rather because he is the Creator and whatever he does with his creation is righteous.

Paul presents a speculation saying, "What if God, although willing to demonstrate His wrath and make His power known, endured with much patience vessels of wrath prepared for destruction?"[170] Now Paul's speculation is certainly true, but he presents it in a way that demonstrates God's purposes belong to God alone and cannot be judged by men. In fact, earlier in the passage Paul quoted Exodus where God told Moses, "I WILL HAVE MERCY ON WHOM I WILL HAVE MERCY, AND I WILL HAVE COMPASSION ON WHOM I WILL HAVE COMPASSION."[171] Paul is telling the Romans that God has his own reasons, and it is not man's place to judge him. Sitting in a position of judging God is brazenly attempting to usurp his throne. It was for that sin that God cast Satan out of heaven, and for that sin, that men and angels will be tormented for eternity.

We will have questions, but the answers to those questions must rest in faith in the absolute sovereignty of God and the truth of Scripture. We do not need to understand everything. We cannot understand everything. Understanding everything would not help us respond to God's love anyway. Full understanding would preempt our faith, and ultimately it is faith that God requires of us. What we can understand and what we must understand is that man is under the wrath of God. Man has been in this condition since Adam sinned in the Garden of Eden. Nevertheless, God has provided for us an alternative to wrath. In his love for man, he sent his Son to take upon himself the sins of the entire world. Receiving this salvation by faith, we will escape the wrath that is still to come, but if we do not obey the Son, as John the Baptist said, the wrath of God will abide upon us. The wrath of God will be fully revealed at the return of Jesus Christ. John the Baptist's expectations will not be disappointed when the Day of the Lord comes.

Believers look forward to a new heaven and a new earth. In this new heaven and earth our resurrection bodies and renewed spirits will be completely fulfilled according to the riches of God's glory. Unbelievers, however, will experience only the fearsome and eternal wrath of God.

---

[170] Romans 9:22 (NASB)
[171] Romans 9:15 (NASB)

## CHAPTER 7—TODAY

*"Is it tomorrow yet?"*— Daniel age 3
*"Valentine's is a day for giving something other than beef."*— Claire age 4
*"When I grow up, I want to be a fire truck"*— Daniel age 3

So, how do we live today? Knowing that this life is temporal, and knowing that we do not belong to ourselves but that we belong to Christ, How should we live? Paul tells us to "Work out your salvation with fear and trembling."[172] We cannot take our spiritual life lightly. There is simply too much at risk to be flippant or casual. The creation in which we live is an awesome place. We are glorious creatures because God created us in his image. All the glory of creation points to its Creator. It is for his benefit that all things exist. We need to center our lives upon this foundation. Our lives exist for him.

Sometimes Christians think that God exists for their personal benefit. Their view of God is something akin to a genie in a bottle. They are the master and he is the benevolent slave who serves at their whim. Of course, there are benefits to worshipping God, but we are made by him and for him: not vice versa. When Cara and Daniel were little, a song was popular for Sunday worship. I do not know whether churches still sing it. It was taken from Hosea chapter 6 which says:

---

[172] Philippians 2:12 (NASB)

# Chapter 7

> Come, let us return to the LORD.
> He has torn us to pieces but he will heal us;
> He has injured us but he will bind our wounds.
> After two days he will revive us;
> On the third day he will restore us,
> That we may live in his presence.
> Let us acknowledge the LORD;
> Let us press on to acknowledge him.
> As surely as the sun rises,
> He will appear.
> He will come to us like the winter rains,
> Like the spring rains that water the earth.[173]

It was a pretty song; I remember, but the problem with the song, and the problem with the passage, is that Israel and Judah quoted here have not repented. They say, "let us press on to acknowledge him," but they do not repent from their sins. They have an attitude as if God exists for their benefit. They take God and his blessings for granted, ". . . as surely as the sun rises, he will appear." They are arrogant and self-absorbed. God says through the prophet, "Your love is like the morning mist, like the early dew that disappears." In the rest of the book, Hosea pronounces God's judgment that is coming because of their insincerity. God will destroy them, but he will also redeem them. He will preserve a remnant. Those who repent will be healed and restored.

I have said for several years, that in the Creation, God made man in his image, and ever since the fall, man has been trying to re-make God in his. I have joked that a best-selling Christian book could be titled, *How to Manipulate God for Fun and Profit*. God, however, cannot be manipulated. He does not flex at our sense of fairness. He does not justify his ways to our reasoning. He is not a genie in a lamp or a slave to our whim and desires. We exist for him. He created us; we did not conjure him. Our attitude toward God reflects our understanding of who he is. What attitude are we supposed to have? Paul tells the Philippians,

> Your attitude should be the same as Christ Jesus: Who, being in very nature God, did not consider equality with God something to

---
[173] Hosea 6:1-3 (NIV)

# Today

be grasped, but made himself nothing, taking the very nature of a servant, being made in human likeness. And being found in appearance as a man, he humbled himself and became obedient to death—even death on a cross![174]

Jesus is our model, our example, and we are supposed to be like him: obedient unto death. Obedience, we now know, is not compliance with sets of rules, regulations, and rote ceremonial acts. We are free from the law, but only because we have died to the flesh on the cross in Christ Jesus. We now have the Holy Spirit as our life, our light, our conscience, and our comforter. If Jesus, who is the Creator of the universe, could humble himself and become a man, and as a man endure God's punishment for sin for all mankind, then how can we presume to live for ourselves: for our own pleasure and glory? We must die to those desires.

Obedience today means seeking God's will earnestly by faith just as Jesus prayed before the crucifixion, ". . . may your will be done." It may be easier to follow a set of rules. Rules provide boundaries that people can see. If you are obeying the rules then family, friends, and coworkers can observe and confirm that you are following the rules. Your attitude does not matter too much as long as you do not cross the line. The problem with rules is that as simple as they are, we cannot keep them. The law did not bring life; it brought death. "The sting of death is sin, and the power of sin is the law."[175] If the Law could have resulted in righteousness, then Jesus would not have needed to die for sins.

Life in the Spirit is genuine; it is not based on outward appearances that people can judge. Paul said that he did not even judge himself, although he was not aware of obvious sin, because his personal standard would be irrelevant anyway. Life in the Spirit is a relationship, not a program or a ritual. Sometimes life in the Spirit finds us feeling lonely, deserted, confused, angry, and frightened. David cries out in the Psalms,

Hear my cry, O God;<br>
Attend unto my prayer.<br>
From the end of the earth will I cry unto thee,

---

[174] Philippians 2:5-11 (NIV)
[175] 1 Corinthians 15:56 (NIV)

# Chapter 7

*When my heart is overwhelmed:*
*Lead me to the rock that is higher than I.*[176]

Paul cried out to God when a messenger of Satan afflicted him. Jesus said to him, "My grace is sufficient for you, for my power is made perfect in weakness."[177] Life in the Spirit is not always easy. Jesus anguished in the Garden of Gethsemane, and we too will anguish over the difficulties that faith presents us. The answer is always the same. Die to the flesh and be alive to God. Place his will above your will. Resurrection follows crucifixion.

Only once in my life have I heard the audible voice of God. While I have witnessed amazing things that can only be attributed to God's intervention, and while I have felt led by the Holy Spirit on many occasions, only once can I remember the audibly present or conversational voice of God. It was a time when I was unemployed; the economy was bad; I was young and uneducated. I was unqualified for many jobs, and the jobs for which I was qualified required me to compete with hundreds of others who were equally or more qualified than I was.

I was afraid. Lisa was afraid. Cara and Daniel were young children. I think even they were afraid. I did whatever work was available. Sometimes the work was manual labor in construction. I swept floors; I helped build fences or decks. I did not have enough tools, and I could not afford to buy them, so I was always the lowest paid laborer.

Sometimes I would work with moving companies packing boxes or loading trucks. My back would sometimes spasm in the middle of the day and I would still work although I could hardly breathe. Still despite my efforts, there was not enough work, or there was not enough pay. Friends who used Scripture to make their point, criticized me, "Paul says, 'If anyone does not provide for his relatives, and especially for his immediate family, he had denied the faith and is worse than an unbeliever.'"[178] Of course, they pulled the Scripture out of the context where it refers to men who were *unwilling* to take care of the widows in their family; it did not refer to the working poor. Nevertheless, I was hurting deeply and embarrassed to be alive.

I returned an unsolicited call from a deacon of the church we attended. I remember I was standing at a pay phone in Raytown or Lee's Summit,

---

[176] Psalm 61:1-2 (KJV)
[177] 2 Corinthians 12:9 (NIV)
[178] 1 Timothy 5:8 (NIV)

# Today

Missouri returning his call. That day I was driving a van on the way to pack a house somewhere in the eastern suburbs of KC. The van had no tags; it had bad brakes, and the person I was working with was smoking marijuana on our way to the job site. This could have already qualified as one of the worst days of my life to that point.

The deacon asked me about my financial and work situation, and I told him. He then told me that the reason he had asked me to call was that he and the other deacons had decided that they would *not* help. I was stunned. I had not asked him for help, but he had gone out of his way, and he made me go out of my way, to inform me that there would be no help coming from the church. I was not even angry. I was just stunned. I did not want a handout. I wanted a job. I was not sitting idle, I was trying to obey Scripture that said, "Whatever you do, work at it with all your heart, as working for the Lord, not for men."[179] I trusted that if I worked my hardest at what God had given me to do that God would make up the difference. Now without my asking for help, my plight was the topic of gossip among men in the church; and they felt compelled not to help and to inform me of their decision.

In the 23rd Psalm, David says, "Even though I walk through the valley of the shadow of death, I will fear no evil, for you are with me; your rod and staff, they comfort me."[180] We often read this familiar Psalm as a comfort, but we need to ask, why did the psalmist find himself in the valley of the shadow of death? The answer: *He was in the valley of the shadow of death because his shepherd, the Lord, had led him there.* We often attribute hard circumstances to our own stupidity and failures, and this can be true. Nevertheless, regardless of our mistakes God is still in control. He is still leading us. Paul, after making a strategic mistake, praised God saying, "Thanks be to God, who always leads us in triumphal procession in Christ."[181] Our failures still result in God's triumph. That does not mean that our path is not painful. Nevertheless, we should not fear the pain. His triumph will prevail. At this time in my life, the Spirit was leading me to a place I would not have chosen to go.

Months later, I was working with a repairperson; he was abusive and vile. I endured cold, hunger, difficult and dangerous work, poor wages,

---

[179] Colossians 3:23 (NIV)
[180] Psalm 23:4 (NIV)
[181] 2 Corinthians 2:14 (NIV)

threats, and endless stories of his sexual abuse of women. I spent long days with him; he did not pay me for all the hours. I do not recall how long I worked for him, but one day I snapped. I quit. I walked out of the house in which we were working and I drove home.

I felt hopeless. Here I had told God that I would do any work to provide for my family, that I would work hard, and do all that he put in front of me as if I was working for him, and now I'd quit a paying job because I was too weak. I quit because I could not take the abuse. I had no one to call. I had no one to turn to.

It may have been that evening or another soon after, but the pressure was intense. Cara and Daniel were asleep. Lisa, too, had gone to bed, but I knew she was not sleeping. I sat in the living room and I cried. I wanted direction. I wanted resolution.

I cried, "God, I need to hear your voice. Tell me what to do!"

Without hesitating, he said to me, "Go and comfort Lisa."

I said, "No, I need to hear your voice!"

He said again, "Go and comfort Lisa because she is just as afraid as you are." Then there was silence.

At that moment, I realized what had just happened. I had cried out to God, I had asked to hear his voice, and he had answered me. The voice was real; it was conversational; it was kind. He had told me what to do, in an audible voice, and I had argued with him saying I needed to *hear* him!

I went to bed, held Lisa, and comforted her. I was comforted now; I had cried out to God and he answered me. He had not told me any grand plan, but he told me what to do next. That was all I needed to know at that moment. It is an awesome thing to realize that God is intimately aware of your circumstance and cares.

The next day I told Lisa what had happened, she told me that she, too, had prayed, and God had told her that I would get a job for $9/hour. That was significantly more than I had made on a regular basis for a long, long time. That evening the phone rang, and a friend asked me if I had ever done any painting. I had. He told me to come to the job site where he had been working and speak to the general contractor. He told me that they paid up to $8/hour. When I showed up the next day, the contractor asked me how much I got for painting and I said with confidence $9/hour.

## Today

Those most difficult times were many years ago, and I suppose there were many lessons learned. The most valuable lesson, however, is that God directed my path even through difficult circumstances. Moreover, the course of my life hinged on that encounter with God. At my weakest moment, God was strong in me. His strength made me complete in my weakness. I surrender much more quickly now. "It's Monday morning, I give up! Lord, have mercy on me today. Give me strength, today." Paul, who had harder experiences than we have ever faced, says,

> I will boast all the more gladly about my weaknesses, so that
> Christ's power may rest on me. That is why, for Christ's sake, I
> delight in weaknesses, in insults, in hardships, in persecutions, in
> difficulties. For when I am weak, then I am strong.[182]

In Philippians 4 Paul describes being content in any situation. If he is hungry, he is content. If he is in need, he is content. Then he says, "I can do everything through him who gives me strength."[183] Paul is not talking about personal ambition. He is talking about enduring hardship. He can be weak, because God makes him strong. In Revelation 3 Jesus talks to the church that is in Philadelphia, he says, "I know your deeds. See I have placed before you an open door that no one can shut. I know that you have little strength, yet you have kept my word and have not denied my name." To this church, there is no warning or criticism. Jesus knows they are weak. He will be strong for them. He knows they are persecuted, so he promises to keep them "from the hour of trial that is going to come upon the whole world." He tells them, "Hold on to what you have, so that no one will take your crown." [184]

Lisa used to play a recording of Twila Paris singing, *Let No Man Take Your Crown*. Cara's young ears took what she heard in Twila's twang and applied what was familiar from her own hand, the result was, "Let no one take your *crayon*." This was not surprising from the lips of the little girl who once recited, "Mirror, mirror, on the wall, who's the fairest of the *mall?*" Jesus' admonition to the churches was simple, and perhaps Cara understood this much: he demands faithfulness.

Faithfulness is not march-step obedience to a religious creed or institutional rules. Religious hierarchies are a form of legalism; consequently,

---
[182] 2 Corinthians 12:9-10 (NIV),
[183] Philippians 4:13 (NIV)
[184] Revelation 3:8, 10, 11 (NIV)

## Chapter 7

they do not convey the truth of the resurrection. Paul called his fellow Apostles, Peter, James, and John, *those in Jerusalem who seemed to be something*. He then said that it made "no difference" because "God shows no partiality."[185] Faithfulness to Jesus Christ does include obedience to divine order. We obey the government, for instance. Paul called civil authority a "minister of God to you for good."[186] God works through governments for our benefit; nevertheless, no one and no thing intervenes in our relationship with Jesus Christ. We will not answer to a church institution on the Day of Judgment. Rather, we will answer to him who paid the price for our salvation.

To the church of Smyrna, Jesus says, "I know your afflictions and your poverty—yet you are rich!"[187] To Philadelphia he said, "I know that you have little strength, yet you have not denied my name." Jesus does not rebuke these two churches. They are hardly shining castles on a hill. They are oppressed and pressured. In Smyrna, some will be murdered for their faith. Jesus commends these churches. Those in weakness will by faith witness his power!

Of the other churches in Asia he says, "You have forsaken your first love . . . You have people there who hold the teaching of Balaam . . . You also have those who hold the teaching of the Nicolaitans . . . You tolerate that woman Jezebel . . . You have a reputation of being alive, but you are dead . . . You say, 'I am rich; I have acquired wealth and do not need a thing.' But you do not realize that you are wretched, pitiful, poor, blind and naked." These are serious rebukes; what would he say to the modern church today? Who is our first love? Whom do we worship? Whom will we tolerate? Whom do we serve? What do we think we need?

Too often, we are concerned about buildings, programs, and finances as if these things mattered. Jude says, "Contend earnestly for the faith which was once for all handed down to the saints."[188] Yet nowhere does the faith require buildings, programs, or finances. Almost nothing material is essential. That is why Jesus promised that God would provide us food and clothing in Matthew 6 (Even in our poorest weeks, we have always had food

---

[185] Galatians 2:6 (NASB)
[186] Romans 13:4 (NASB)
[187] Revelation 2:9 (NIV)
[188] Jude 3 (NASB)

# Today

and clothing). When the church becomes self-obsessed then it has left its first love. We need to focus on Jesus Christ rather than on some facility, program, or organization. Churches fall in love with doing church, people fall in love with pastors or leaders and a type of idolatry emerges.

Churches attempting to influence society through political activism are in error. In the *Parable of the Weeds* in Matthew 13 Jesus tells us to let the weeds grow together with the wheat until the time of harvest. In the parable, the field is the *world*. The harvesters, who are angels and not men, will separate the wheat from the weeds on the day of harvest. We cannot pull weeds without damaging wheat. The Christian has longer-lasting influence as a messenger of the Gospel than he will ever have as a politician, lobbyist, or protester.

A long time ago, I attended a so-called Christian university. On Saturday night, the pastoral students would go to another town to do street ministry. My roommate was in the program, and so I went with him. We arrived at a street not far from the town's center. Up the hill and bathed in spotlights was a splendid colonial architecture church building. At the bottom of the hill nearest the town square were shanty taverns. The contrast reminded me of Jesus' rebuke of the Pharisees where he called them "whited sepulchres."[189] They looked beautiful on the outside, but on the inside, they were full of death and decay. Likewise, the beautiful church stood lifeless while the seedy taverns were crowded with men that had spiritual needs.

Across the street from the bars, the young preachers began setting up their mobile PA systems on the roofs of their cars. Then they started shouting damnation to the men and boys who were drinking inside. It seemed to me that this was likely to incite a riot; I expected the police to come and arrest us all. I about panicked until someone explained to me that the police condoned the preacher boys' practice because the dispensing of shame kept the people inside the taverns and off the streets.

Thankfully, my roommate, Bill, was also uncomfortable with the scene. He and I started walking away from *East Church Street* and started intercepting young men on their way to the taverns. Most would stop to visit with us. When they would listen, we shared the Gospel. One at least believed. In subsequent weeks, we had a Bible study in his parents' home. We sat

---

[189] Matthew 23:27 (KJV)

around a wood burning stove built from a 55-gallon drum. The gentle couple told us how their son used to drink excessively every Saturday night, but now he did not. They told us how he now rode to and from work in the back of a pickup every weekday for over half an hour each way. He covered up with a canvas tarp to keep from freezing, and he read the Bible that we had given him. His parents had been praying for him, and they saw their prayers answered.

The last time I accompanied the group of preachers was a few weeks later. Bill and I had returned from the cozy Bible study, and the preachers were packing up their sound gear. While they were packing their gear, an intoxicated man approached me. He was angry. I do not know why he came to me. Maybe I simply made eye contact when no one else would, but he was angry. He yelled at me, pointing into the crowd of preachers, "He promised me a sandwich!"

I asked, "He promised you what?" I was not sure what I was hearing.

He said, "He said that if I listened, he would buy me a sandwich."

I smiled, looked at Bill, and then said to the old man, "I'll buy you a sandwich." The three of us walked to a diner around the corner on South Main, and I ordered him a cheeseburger, fries, and coffee. I am not sure anyone actually promised him anything. I *am* sure that he thought someone had promised him a sandwich.

After we returned to campus, the leaders kicked Bill and me off the team. Whatever they shouted through those PA systems did not express the love that God has for sinful man. In retrospect, I doubt that buying the man a sandwich was sufficient either.

In Jesus' ministry, you find him addressing the physical needs of people, but meeting physical needs was not his primary goal. Sometimes he would not feed them. He wanted them to hear the gospel of the kingdom. He wanted men to know who he was. He wanted them to know that he loved them. He wanted to save them.

Jesus wants us to show his love to a lost world not to condemn the world. The time is coming when God will judge all men. We need not worry about hurrying it along. Judging sinners, pulling the weeds, is not the ministry of the Christian. Rather we are to reflect Jesus' attitude.

# Today

When Jesus looked out over Jerusalem as he arrived for Passover, he wept for the city. He had compassion on men even though he knew that within a few days they would crucify him. If we cannot weep with compassion for the sinner, we should keep our mouths shut and our public address systems turned off. God loves people.

God loved us *all* when he formed Adam from the earth. He loved us individually as he breathed into Adam the breath of life. He loved us after we fell into sin. He loved us when we nailed his hands and feet to the cross. He loved us when we crowned him with thorns. He loved us when we exposed his naked body and cast lots for his clothing. He loved us when we mocked him, spit on him, and hit him. He loved us as he struggled to breathe on the cross. He loved us even as our sin infected his holy body. He loved us although it cost him his life.

Christians responding to his love should reach out to the poor and to the brokenhearted. Christians responding to his love should meet the physical needs of others. When confronted with a beggar in the street, Christians should ask themselves, what would Jesus have me do? Matthew 5:42 tells us, but I think you can guess.

James, the brother of Jesus, gives an example of true ministry, "Religion that God our Father accepts as pure and faultless is this: to look after orphans and widows in their distress and to keep oneself from being polluted by the world."[190] This is relational, not bureaucratic. It is compassionate, not adversarial. Sometimes according to Jude, it can be confrontational: mercy mixed with fear. Even so, it is always personal and never institutional. Paul wrote letters to people he knew. He sent Timothy and Titus to work personally with churches when he could not be present. The Gospel is always relational. John emphasized to his "dear children" that they should love one another.

Throughout life, whether you find yourself with a small group of believers, or within some larger group, remember that an institution cannot nurture spiritual life. The institution is not the objective, although it usually tries to be. Jesus did not come to earth to start a corporation. He came to save people. Our spiritual life is refreshed when we interact with people, but it suffocates in religious hierarchies. Jesus told his disciples, "Do not be

---

[190] James 1:27 (NIV)

called leaders, for one is your leader, *that is*, Christ."[191] To men like Stephanas, Paul urged the Corinthians to submit. He goes on to add, "And to everyone who joins in the work, and labors at it."[192] To paraphrase, Paul said, *obey everyone who works for the cause of the Gospel.* That is hardly hierarchical. With the Spirit's guidance, it is cooperative and relational. Without the Spirit, it would be chaos, and that is why institutions organize in hierarchies.

Relationships with believers are important; gathering small groups in Jesus' name brings him into the midst (Matthew 18:20). The Gospel, the message of his great love, can change lives, it can heal, it can comfort, it can encourage, it can cleanse. It brings life, not resuscitation, not prolonged dying; it brings resurrection!

The early church met together weekly to celebrate the Lord's Supper as a full meal. There was the cup and the one loaf of bread. The fellowship around dinner bonded people together more closely than family. Paul wrote to the Corinthians saying, "Because there is one loaf, we, who are many, are one body, for we all partake of the one loaf."[193] The fellowship of the Lord's Supper created unity within the body in a way that meeting together to sing songs and sermonize cannot do.

Different people can attend the same church for years without even knowing each other at all. This is not what John had in mind when he implored his dear children to love one another. Love exists on a personal, not a corporate level.

Whether we are among believers or unbelievers, our only message is the message of the Gospel. Jesus, the Creator God, the Son of God, the Word of God, is equal to God the Father. Man fell under God's judgment by sinning against God. Jesus humbled himself, became a man through the virgin birth. Being born without sin, he lived a sinless life and fulfilled all the law. Being obedient to the Father, he endured the cross for our sakes. He, who had no sin, was made to be sin, so that sin could be judged in his body by the sacrifice of his blood on the cross. He gave up his life as a propitiation for the sins of the world. He entered the Most Holy Place before the throne of God in

---

[191] Matthew 23:10 (NASB)
[192] 1 Corinthians 16:16 (NIV)
[193] 1 Corinthians 10:17 (NIV)

# Today

heaven bringing with him the sacrifice of his blood. God's righteous judgment was satisfied, and God raised him to life.

Those accepting forgiveness of sins and the gift of eternal life share with him the cross in order to die to sin and become alive to God through faith. Because he rose again, we too have the hope and assurance of the resurrection to come. We can face all hardship and endure all pain through Christ who strengthens us. This is our message both to believers and to the world, if we continue in the faith that saved us.

If people understood this, they would not live in sexual immorality. If young women understood this, they would not murder their offspring in abortion clinics. If doctors understood this, they would not sacrifice the unborn on the modern altars of Baal. If the media understood this, they would not produce or sell pornography. If businessmen understood this, they would not defraud their customers and investors. If politicians understood this, they would not defame the marriage institution by sanctioning homosexual relationships. If substance abusers understood this, they would choose their Savior over their chemicals. If husbands understood this, they would love their wives. If wives understood this, they would honor their husbands. If children understood this, they would obey their parents. If we understood this, we would love people; we would be extravagant with our giving and sharing. We would share our lives together with other believers as a single body. If we understood this, we would need no set of rules: we would follow the Spirit.

We live in a wicked world. Injustice abounds. We can become discouraged at the darkness that surrounds us, and we can become anxious and strike out against the symptoms of sin. We still can choose whether to wrestle against flesh and blood, or whether to obey God and his Word. We can attempt to reform society by imposing a religious fascism upon it or we can carry the refreshing Gospel of Jesus Christ to a parched and dying world. We can march out and try to rip the weeds from the field, but if we do, we will damage the wheat. The cross of Jesus Christ solved once-for-all man's problem with sin. Our attempts at social reformation only distract from the truth. We cannot reform the sinner, but the Gospel can.

Striking out against the symptoms of man's sinful nature is futile; it is like picking ticks in Missouri; it is like swatting flies in Iowa, or slapping mosquitoes in Minnesota. Treating the symptoms ignores the cure. Treating the symptoms is applying the law: it can only bring guilt and death. The Gospel of Jesus Christ, on the other hand, brings eternal life.

Every year different methodologies emerge that promise the implementer a happier life, a more successful marriage, or a more fulfilling career if only the reader would follow certain *spiritual* principals. Christian bookstores are full of this garbage. Paul says of the various systems,

> These are all destined to perish with use, because they are based on human commands and teachings. Such regulations indeed have an appearance of wisdom, with their self-imposed worship, their false humility and their harsh treatment of the body, but they lack any value in restraining sensual indulgence.[194]

*Sensual indulgence* does not necessarily mean sexual gratification. It means self-gratification. These seemingly Christian psychologies are ever popular because they appear to meet people where they live and promise solutions to *real* problems. They make people *feel* better, although they cannot produce righteousness. They are deceptions. Rather than restraining sensual indulgences, pseudo-spirituality panders to it. Behavioral psychology might teach people how to live in *this* life, but it will not get them into the next one. Jesus asked, "What good will it be for a man if he gains the whole world, yet forfeits his soul? Or what can a man give in exchange for his soul?"[195] What good is it if a man is happier, more successful in his marriage, and more fulfilled in his job, if he never comes to faith in Jesus Christ and only lives to gratify himself?

What must we do? How shall we live? Jesus says, "If anyone would come after me, he must deny himself and take up his cross and follow me."[196] Resurrection follows crucifixion, and we hope for it by faith. Some people expect a reward now as if gratifying themselves in this life is the goal. They take the attitude, *he who dies with the most tangible blessings wins!* (Wins what?) They see gaining physical assets as affirmation that they are on the right track. We should be looking beyond temporal rewards (self-gratification) and clinging to the hope of eternity.

---

[194] Colossians 2:22, 23 (NIV)
[195] Matthew 16:26 (NIV)
[196] Matthew 16:24 (NIV)

# Today

Claire is home-schooled, and the question about socializing with peers arises occasionally. I do not reply with a schedule of Claire's social activities; regardless of how much time she spends with kids, she spends more time with adults. My answer to people is simply this; we spend most of our lives relating to adults (because we all grow up). What is more important, learning to relate to your childhood peers or learning to relate to adults? Likewise, our eternity will be infinitely longer than our lives on earth. Upon what should we be focusing? Where would we prefer to be comfortable, here or there?

When Daniel was a little guy, he was always fascinated by what was happening tomorrow. Consequently, he would always be asking, "Is it tomorrow, yet?" It puzzled him that the answer was always, "No, not yet." Time still confuses us, but eventually we will not worry about time.

Hebrews 4 explains that God appointed a holy day for the children of Israel, the Sabbath day. It was a day during which they were to acknowledge their Creator. For us there is also an appointed day during which we, too, acknowledge our Creator. If we think that day is Sunday, then our odds of being correct are 14.29%. The writer of Hebrews says, "Therefore God again set a certain day, calling it Today, when a long time later he spoke through David, as was said before: 'Today, if you hear his voice, do not harden your hearts.'"[197]

The writer of Hebrews also says, "Encourage one another daily, as long as it is called Today, so that none of you may be hardened by sin's deceitfulness."[198] No, Daniel, it is not tomorrow yet. *Today* is the day we have. *Today* is the day that God has appointed to us. *Today* matters. We look forward to Jesus' return when we will enter eternity where there is no longer a today or tomorrow as we measure time; but *Today* is when we must respond.

Claire, when worrying about what might happen on Valentine's Day, declared so very wisely, "Valentine's is a day for giving something other than beef." No one is sure what she meant, but her conviction was genuine. Likewise, *Today* is a day for living for something other than our selfish desires. *Today* is the day to acknowledge our Creator and Redeemer. *Today* is the day we die to self and live for him. *Today* is the day we encourage one

---
[197] Hebrews 4:7 (NIV)
[198] Hebrews 3:13 (NIV)

another in him. Just as God commanded Israel to remember their Creator each Sabbath, so we, too, remember him *Today*.

This is not psychology. This is not human achievement. It cannot be packaged, marketed, and distributed. It cannot be bought or sold, but it can be acquired. It cannot be taught, but it can be learned. It does not guarantee health, wealth, peace, prosperity, or even safety. It *does* promise trials. It is a relationship of faith; knowing also that faith is tested and refined.

Some teach that faith is a cosmic spiritual power that we tap into and use to gratify our own desires. This teaching elevates man and ignores the Creator. True faith is trusting God for everything regardless of circumstance or specific outcomes.

Jude, the brother of Jesus, writes a short letter reminding people that God will judge the wicked and encouraging believers to persevere in their faith. He says,

> "In the last times there will be scoffers who will follow their own ungodly desires." These are the men who divide you, who follow mere natural instincts and do not have the Spirit. But you, dear friends, build yourselves up in your most holy faith and pray in the Holy Spirit. Keep yourselves in God's love as you wait for the mercy of our Lord Jesus Christ to bring to you eternal life. Be merciful to those who doubt; snatch others from the fire and save them; to others show mercy, mixed with fear—hating even the clothing stained by corrupted flesh.
>
> > To him who is able to keep you from falling
> > and to present you before his glorious presence
> > without fault and with great joy—
> > to the only God our Savior
> > be glory, majesty, power and authority,
> > through Jesus Christ our Lord,
> > before all ages,
> > now and forevermore!
> > Amen[199]

---

[199] Jude 18-25 (NIV)

**Today**

Dearest Cara, Daniel, Claire, and Gabrielle:

As I finish writing to you, I confess, "Surely I spoke of things I did not understand, Things too wonderful for me to know."[200] Consequently, examine the Scripture and confirm, ". . . whether these things [are] so."[201]

My lovely children, before you were born, God gave your mother and me your names as blessings for your lives on earth:

Cara Michal—*Joy, a little river.*
Daniel Shane—*God is my judge; God is gracious.*
Claire Maddison—*Bright and shining warrior.*
Gabrielle Sophia—*Messenger of God's wisdom.*

I have written this book for your sakes so that you will strengthen your foundation in Jesus Christ, so that you will resist deception, and so that you will be a blessing to others. As Jesus said, "It is more blessed to give than to receive."[202] The blessings we have, and the blessings we receive are not given for our self-gratification, but rather they given to us so we will bless others.

I pray for you always asking God to accomplish in your lives the blessings of your names. Jesus tells the believers in the struggling church of Pergamum,

To him who overcomes<br>
I will give some of the hidden manna.<br>
I will also give him a white stone<br>
with a new name written on it,<br>
known only to him who receives it.[203]

I pray that the blessings of your names will be fulfilled in your lives, but more importantly, I pray that you will each overcome by faith and receive from Jesus the blessing of your *new* name, a name portending all that God has prepared for you in eternity.

Love,

Dad

---

[200] Job 42:3 (NIV)
[201] Acts 17:11 (NASB)
[202] Acts 20:35 (NASB)
[203] Revelation 2:17 (NIV)

# References

[i] Shelley, Percy Bysshe "Ozymandius" 13 July 2007
  < http://www.online-literature.com/shelley_percy/672/>

[ii] The Incredibles, Pixar Animation Studios, DVD, Disney, 2005

[iii] Frost, Robert "Provide, Provide" 13 July 2007
  <http://www.online-literature.com/frost/740/>.

[iv] Springsteen, Bruce "Glory Days" 13 July 2007
  <http://www.oldielyrics.com/lyrics/bruce_springsteen/glory_days.html>.

[v] Frost, Robert "Out, Out" 13 July 2007
  <http://www.online-literature.com/frost/752/>.

[vi] Shakespeare, William "Macbeth, Act V, Scene 5" 13 July 2007
  <http://www.online-literature.com/view.php/macbeth/26?term=out, out>

[vii] Blake, William "The Lamb" 13 July 2007
  <http://www.online-literature.com/blake/619/>.

[viii] Frost, Robert "Death of a Hired Man" 13 July 2007
  <http://www.online-literature.com/frost/752/>

[ix] Longfellow, Henry Wadsworth "Psalm of Life" 13 July 2007
  <http://www.online-literature.com/henry_longfellow/942/>.

[x] Lewis, C.S. The Lion, the Witch, and the Wardrobe (New York: Harper Collins, 1994) 156:189.

[xi] Eddinger, Terry W., "Wine in Ancient Israel",
  Biblical Illustrator, Volume 30, Number 2

[xii] Wesley, Charles "Amazing Love" 13 July 2007
  <http://www.lyricsday.com/
  John_Wesley-Amazing_Love_Lyrics-lyrics-36666310.html>

[xiii] Negro Spiritual, "Were You There" Lutheran Hymnal 13 July 2007
  <http://www.lutheran-hymnal.com/lyrics/lw505.htm>

www.ingramcontent.com/pod-product-compliance
Lightning Source LLC
Chambersburg PA
CBHW020003050426
42450CB00005B/296